CARL!

THE STORY OF AN AMERICAN HERO

by
John Devaney

BANTAM BOOKS
TORONTO • NEW YORK • LONDON • SYDNEY • AUCKLAND

Photo of Lewis home courtesy of John Devaney. Other photos courtesy of Wide World, Inc.

Cover photograph by Benoit/Courtesy of Wide World Photos, Inc.

Book Design by David M. Nehila

CARL! THE STORY OF AN AMERICAN HERO

A Bantam Book / August 1984

Produced by Cloverdale Press, Inc.
133 Fifth Avenue, New York, N.Y. 10003

Typography by ILNY Communications and Media Corporation

ISBN 0-553-25005-1

Published simultaneously in the United States and Canada

Bantam Books are published by Bantam Books, Inc. Its trademark, consisting of the words "Bantam Books" and the portrayal of a rooster, is Registered in U.S. Patent and Trademark Office and in other countries. Marca Registrada. Bantam Books, Inc., 666 Fifth Avenue, New York, New York 10103.

PRINTED IN THE UNITED STATES OF AMERICA

H 0 9 8 7 6 5 4 3 2 1

GOING FOR FOUR

Carl Lewis won the 100-meter final at the American Trials, thus ensuring Olympic berths in that event and the 4 × 100-meter relay. Then he won the long-jump final and he was guaranteed a chance to win three Olympic gold medals. Finally, he set his sights on the 200 meters.

He won the two 200 heats. On Thursday afternoon, June 21, ABC-TV cameras sent the race live to an expectant America. Carl knelt into the starting blocks, arms straining against the salmon-pink artificial track surface. At the gun the eight runners bolted into the curve. Kirk Baptiste, the U.S. collegiate champion, had the lead, but when the ragged line came out of the curve into the straightaway, Carl had forged ahead. He beat Baptiste by two yards. His time, 19.86 seconds, was Carl's third best ever, but that was not uppermost in his mind as he bounded happily down the track. He told the nation what was first in his mind as he raised his right hand and showed four fingers.

Four! He had gone for four! And he had made four!

He fell to both knees and kissed the track, thanking God, he said later, for the gifts he had been given—and what he had done with those gifts. Could he win four golds at the Olympics and be the new Jesse Owens? "I want to be considered the first Carl Lewis," he said. "The whole Jesse Owens thing is not dead, but I'm doing this because of me and who I am."

Later he told a reporter: "I know what it takes to win. It takes, of course, hard work. It takes careful planning. It takes a spiritual life. It also takes simple relaxation. And right now I have all those elements so I am not afraid."

And Now, It Was on to the Olympic Games.

CONTENTS

For Mary, Carlo, Susan and Marco

PROLOGUE

Holding high the torch, she bounds out of the shadows of the tunnel. She runs onto the track, which glows pink in the heat of the afternoon sun. The 100,000 people, massed high row on row in the oval-shaped coliseum, are standing, their eyes on the smiling runner, who is wearing a white track suit. Her identity has been a secret these past few days before the opening of the 1984 Summer Olympic Games.

Now, as she jogs around the track in front of the 10,000 athletes massed on the green infield, loudspeakers tell her name to a watching world. She is Gina Hemphill, granddaughter of Jesse Owens. She has been selected by the American organizers of these Games to be the one—the last in a relay of 2400 runners—to carry the Olympic torch into the Los Angeles Coliseum. That torch will start the fire that will glow during the two weeks of the Games of the 23rd Olympiad.

For the rangy, 6'3", 185-pound Carl Lewis—standing with the United States team in a sea of red, white, and blue uniforms, his teammates cheering the ghostly white figure as it strides by—this harkening of the memory of Jesse Owens is one last reminder of just how much one nation, *his* nation, expects of Carl Lewis during these two weeks: not just one gold, not two or three, this U.S. of A. yearns for Carl Lewis to win what he himself has promised to win—four gold medals, a total no Olympic track and field athlete ever has won in nearly half a century of trying, not since . . .

Jesse Owens. Jesse, the world's fastest human of his time, the one who raced horses—and beat them. Jesse Owens is one of those American sports heroes like Babe Ruth and Willie Mays whose deeds are told to generation after generation of kids growing up. And so millions of Americans—men and women not even born yet in 1936—have told their children these stories once told to them: how the lithe, soft-spoken Ohio State runner won the 100 meters, the 200 meters, and the long jump, and how he ran the anchor leg for the winning 400-meter U.S. relay team at the 1936 Olympic games in Berlin. There are grandfathers and grandmothers who recall hearing as children how Adolf Hitler, the German dictator, ranted that Black people were an inferior race; and how Hitler had stormed from the Berlin stadium red-faced and fuming, when the Black American Jesse Owens won gold medal after gold medal.

Jesse Owens. In the decades since his accomplishments at Berlin, dozens of "new Jesse Owenses" have come along, determined to win that quartet of gold in long jumping and sprinting—at London in 1948, Helsinki in 1952, Melbourne in 1956, Rome in 1960, Tokyo in 1964, Mexico City in 1968, Munich in 1972, Montréal in 1976, Moscow in 1980. Not one could be the sprinter fast enough or the leaper strong enough to survive heats, semifinals and finals to win all four events.

And now there is Carl Lewis, 23 years old, as big and fast as a football running back, as springy and soaring a leaper as a basketball rebounder, so tall and fast and strong that European sports writers call him "Superman." Once he had been "the runt" in a family of athletes and once he had feared he would always be a loser. But during the past two years he has told first himself, then the people he loved, and finally the world, that yes, he could be the new Jesse Owens—or perhaps the new Carl Lewis, a legend himself. Now, as Gina Hemphill sprints by him and his teammates, it is as though the ghost of Jesse Owens has come here to watch, along with the rest of the spectators, a time of testing for Carl Lewis.

CHAPTER 1

THE EARLY YEARS

1936

. . . The year is 1936. Six runners are crouched on the red cinder track, bodies poised, spikes dug in behind the starting line. A wave of rain sweeps across the stadium, drenching athletes and onlookers alike. But storm clouds cannot dampen the resolve of these Olympic medal hopefuls in the final heat of the 200-meter race. At the starter's gun, six determined men in search of gold burst from their crouching posture on the oval.

It was all over in the twinkling of an eye. Less than 21 seconds told the story of the 200-meter footrace at the Berlin Olympics of

1936. Jesse Owens, the black American athlete extraordinaire, led from the starting line. His teammate, Mack Robinson, brother of baseball great Jackie, finished three or four meters back to take the silver.

Owens's gold in the 200-meter was his third of the '36 Summer Olympics. Under the grudging eye of Chancellor Adolf Hitler, the slim, soft-spoken Ohio State senior had tied the Olympic record in the 100-meter with a time of 10.3 seconds and established a new Olympic best in the broad jump—26 feet, 5²¹⁄₆₄ inches.

Owens would go on to team with fellow Americans Ralph Metcalfe, Foy Draper, and Frank Wykoff in the 400-meter relay. Their first-place finish in that event gave Owens a total of four Olympic golds, quite a blow to Hitler's much-vaunted theory of "Aryan supremacy."

1973

. . . The year is 1973. The scene is Franklin Field, Philadelphia. The occasion is an age-group track meet held in honor of Jesse Owens. A diminutive black twelve-year-old from Willingboro, N.J., wins the long jump, prevailing over a number of taller, more experienced competitors.

The elated young champ, 5′4″ Carl Lewis, is introduced to Olympic great Jesse Owens, who commends him on his performance. "He came over," Lewis recalled recently to *The Runner*, "and said to the other kids, 'You guys should take a lesson from this smaller guy. He was determined and he really tried hard.' It was an inspiration," Lewis recalls.

Lewis's father was also thrilled to make the acquaintance of the graying Olympian. It was not just Owens's Olympic performance that set the man apart for Bill. He recalled how, as a trade school student in Chicago a few years after the Berlin Olympics he had been impressed by Owens's unselfish spirit. "Jesse was working as a district manager for the Pekin cleaners chain," Bill recalled lately in *The New York Times*. "Whenever he stopped at the store, all the kids would gather around him and ask him questions. There was a strip of dirt nearby and he would go over there in his good clothes and demonstrate his sprinter's start for us."

Though he died in 1980, Owens lives on as

an American hero, a model of superb athleticism and high ideals. "And whenever I saw Jesse in the years after that, he remembered," Bill Lewis said. "He would always ask me how Carl was doing."

1984

Eleven years after that memorable meeting—and eleven inches later—6′3″ Carl Lewis stands a good chance of duplicating Owens's legendary Olympic performance. His ascent from that now historic meeting with Owens has been nothing short of meteoric. But it didn't always look that easy . . .

AN ATHLETIC HERITAGE

Evelyn Lawler was the daughter of an Alabama cotton farmer. She attended Tuskegee Institute on a track scholarship and suffered a keen disappointment when she failed to qualify for the 1952 Olympic team as a hurdler. A year earlier she had finished a commendable sixth at the prestigious Pan-American Games.

Evelyn met and married big Bill Lewis from Chicago while they were both students at Tuskegee. Bill was also a talented athlete —a sprinter, long jumper, and football player.

Upon graduation, the Lewises took teaching positions in nearby Birmingham, where son Mackie was born in 1954. Cleveland Lewis arrived in 1956. Carl was born July 1, 1961, and daughter Carol two years later.

WILLINGBORO

With four children, the Lewises decided to make the move to Willingboro, N.J., a pretty suburb of Philadelphia. Willingboro's curving driveways, green lawns, and Cape Cod ranch-style homes are ringed with apple orchards and dairy farms. Bill and Evelyn bought a handsome four-bedroom house, which had a lovely large backyard.

Bill took a job as social science teacher and coach of the girls' track team at nearby John F. Kennedy High. Evelyn taught physical education at Willingboro High and coached their girls' track team. Whenever the girls' track teams from the two schools competed, a friend reports, "Bill and Evelyn kissed and came out fighting."

The Lewis house was just a five-minute run from the vast playing fields at Willingboro High. Carl and Carol often ran it together. The two were inseparable. As adolescents, they stood just about the same height and played most of the same games and sports. "She didn't even socialize with girls until she was thirteen," Carol's mother once said. "She was Carl's buddy and no one else's. His friends were her friends. She played their games. They treated her just like one of them."

The older Lewis kids rapidly established themselves as accomplished athletes at Willingboro High. Mackie became their fastest sprinter, setting a county record in the 220-yard dash. Cleve became top scorer on the high school soccer team.

THE TRACK CLUB

In the summer of 1969 Bill and Evelyn organized the Willingboro Track Club. The club was originally all female, designed to give teenage girls year-round competitive track. But under pressure from high school boys like Mackie and Cleve Lewis, the club soon went co-ed.

Bill and Evelyn worked hard to keep the club alive. They held dances and raffles to raise funds and dipped into their own savings, when necessary, to cover the difference. The club thrived. Within a year the WTC was sponsoring a team to the Jesse Owens novice meets in Philadelphia.

Two of the club's best runners were Mackie and Cleve Lewis. Carl and Carol often tagged along to watch their brothers and the other runners during practices and meets. The youngsters liked to hang around the long jump's sandpit. "We'd build sand castles in the pit and smash them," Carol reported. "Having the two youngest come to meets saved baby-sitting money," mother Evelyn recalls.

At home in their hedge-rimmed backyard, Carl and Carol staged their own track meets. One summer their father bought a pile of sand to build a patio. Ten-year-old Carl and eight-year-old Carol converted the pile into a long-jump pit and leaped into it. They also set up chairs and tables as "hurdles" and competed against each other in their mother's favorite event. Carol often beat Carl. When she won, Carol would run into the house and grab a medal or trophy won by her mother, then return to the backyard for a "victory ceremony." The loser, Carl, glowered.

"THE RUNT"

Watching the two play, Bill Lewis hoped Carl would begin to grow—he was, everyone said, "the runt" of the family. Bill began to wonder if Carl would be the Lewis's non-athlete.

Carl didn't seem to think so. Almost every day he scampered down the long-jump runway at Willingboro High, leaped at the takeoff bar and plopped into the sandpit. "Nobody was into the long jump," he remembers. "So I always had lots of time to practice. I never had to wait my turn. And in the long jump I got to run *and* jump."

Carl learned that the Willingboro High record for the long jump was almost 21 feet, 6 inches. Poised almost every afternoon at the top of the runway, Carl thought about reaching 22 feet and becoming the new record holder. Rarely did he fly more than 7 feet from the takeoff bar, though.

BEAMON'S LEAP

It had been two years earlier, some three years after it happened, when the then ten-year-old Carl first learned of the longest jump in history. At the 1968 Olympics in Mexico City, a stringbeanish jumper from New York City, Bob Beamon, had soared 29 feet, 2½ inches—not 28 feet, which would have broken the record by half a foot, but 29-2½, breaking the record by almost *two* feet. Up to then, 28 feet had been considered a kind of magic barrier. Beamon had arched right through the barrier. He had broken the record not with a bite but with a gulp. "Compared to this jump," an awed Soviet jumper had observed, "we are as children."

Carl thought often about Beamon's leap. One day he went out to his backyard with a tape and measured off 29 feet and 2 inches. He stuck a peg in the grass at 29 feet, 2 inches, then walked back to his starting point. The peg seemed so distant. He wondered how any human being could fly that far through the air.

Carl tried, Lord how he tried. Sometimes after practice he limped home. His right knee ached. He'd fallen down when he was eleven. Scar tissue was scratching the tendon in the right leg, causing a toothache-like pain after he jumped. And, like most jumpers, he leaped off his right foot. The right knee often puffed up as big as a tennis ball.

One day, twelve-year-old Carl walked home tired and in pain, again having lost in a long-jumping competition. "It was frustrating to always be the dud of the family," he said years later. "So I really worked hard. I had to be perfect, to be like they were . . ."

Arriving home, Carl spotted his father and cried out to him in frustration, "I'm tired of losing! I'm tired of losing!" His father smiled and said, "Well, buddy, then the ony thing to do is start winning."

Easily said, but when you're the runt and the dud of the family and you've got a leg that hurts, how do you become a winner?

CHAPTER 2

PANIC TIME

Carl hurried down the corridor at Willingboro High, his long, thin arms swinging. He was wearing tan slacks, jogging shoes, and a track sweater emblazoned with the letter "W." Also written on the sweater were the words "25 feet."

"25 FEET"

A boy stopped him. "Hey, Carl," he asked, "what's '25 feet' mean?"

"That's my goal—25 feet. Before I leave high school I am going to jump 25 feet."

The boy laughed. "No one in this county's ever jumped 25 feet," the boy said.

Carl, a 16-year-old junior on that spring day in 1978, had recently jumped 22 feet to break the school record. And he could feel himself growing taller every day. He stood a stringy 5′10″ and 150 pounds. His older brother, Cleve, a soccer All-American at Brandeis University, had counseled Carl: "One of these days soon you're going to start filling out the way I did at your age."

Though Carl had finally grown taller than his little sister, Carol was still the feisty "me too" kid. "Carol is *not* shy," her mother once said. While Carl was laid back and at times diffident, Carol was ever outspoken, so much so, her mother said, "Sometimes she almost frightens me. Whatever she wants, she goes and gets." And what Carol wanted was whatever Carl wanted. When Carl took music lessons, Carol took music lessons. When Carl joined the school orchestra as a cellist, Carol joined the orchestra. And now that Carl wanted to set records as a long-jumper, Carol wanted to set records as a long-jumper, too. A basketball coach saw her leap and insisted she play for him. No, said Carol, when she entered Willingboro in the fall of '77, she was going out for the long jump.

THE "NEW" CARL

By the fall of 1978, people were talking about the "new" Carl. Just after his seventeenth birthday that July, he had bloomed physically, just as his brother had predicted. Carl now stood a thick-chested, strong-legged six feet and weighed close to 170 pounds. His still-boyish face had the strong hard lines of a piece of carved mahogany. As a senior in the spring of 1979, Carl leaped 25 feet, 9 inches, and now no one laughed when he wore the number 25 on his sweater. Carl had a new goal. Over his bed he mounted a sign that read: "Carl Lewis—King of the 27-foot jumpers." "Maybe," Bill said to Evelyn, "the genes just fell right."

Carl's right knee still ached. He had patella tendinitis, or jumper's knee. He tried to leap off his left foot to ease the pain. No one had ever heard of a jumper taking off on his left foot, the "wrong" foot, but Carl sometimes traveled 25 feet with a "wrong-foot" takeoff. Still, it was difficult switching from right to left and, a few months later, from left to right. "I ended up taking off on the right," he said later. "I was young and I wasn't thinking much of what I was doing."

THE 100-YARD DASH

Because his knee ached, he practiced his long jumping only a few minutes a day. Since the knee didn't hurt when he ran—it was the jarring takeoff that caused the pain—Carl joined the sprinters for the 100-yard dash. Usually he saw only the other boys' heels, his time for the 100 a so-so 10.3 seconds. But during that senior year in the spring of 1979, his long legs began to swallow yards of the green-topped track at Willingboro High. By late spring he was catching everyone, his time a near-U.S. record of 9.5 seconds. And even though he practiced the long jump only a few minutes a day, he had soared 26 feet, 8 inches—a U.S. high school record.

CARL'S GOALS

The once-diffident Carl couldn't hold back—or would he ever again—the pride he felt inside himself. He had been given gifts and he was working to make those gifts shine. "I always had the feeling I was born to do something," he once said of that astonishing growth period between his junior and senior years at Willingboro. "But until then I never knew what it was."

What he wanted to do, it became clear, was to be the world's longest leaper and its fastest human. That was a breadth of achievement that no one had attained since Jesse Owens won the 100-meter race, the 200-meter, the 400-meter relay, and the long jump at the 1936 Olympics. Carl began to speculate on the possibility of making the U.S. team that would be going to the 1980 Olympics in Moscow.

CARL & CAROL

Was Carl destined to be an Olympian in 1980? Then Carol was going to be an Olympian too, she told anyone who would listen. As a sophomore at Willingboro she had leaped close to 20 feet and had fixed her sights on the American women's record of 21½ feet. If Carl could soar 25+ feet, she could surely fly to 22.

Almost every morning senior and sophomore ran the good minute's sprint to school from their suburban home. Both liked to wear what Carl called "good" clothes, bought at boutiques in New York and Philadelphia. Carl walked as erectly as a West Point cadet, arms swinging at his sides. Almost always a smile glowed on his strong face, which triangulated to a long, sharply hewn jaw and a jutting chin. Carl spoke with a charged and bubbling enthusiasm, using words like "whoosh!" "boom!" and—with a clap of his hands—"gone!" to describe one of his leaps or sprints. Still, he said, he was "slow and easy" compared to Carol. "I like to be in *control* of most everything I am doing."

COLLEGE

Carl had the opportunity to choose from many colleges that offered him tuition and board to run and jump for them. He chose the University of Houston, one reason being that the school's trim, silvery-haired coach, Tom Tellez, was considered by many the best coach of jumpers in the nation. One of his pupils had been high-jumper Dwight Stones, an Olympian in 1976.

In the fall of 1979 Carl entered Houston. His oldest brother, Mackie, joined him, studying for a degree in geology. Later Carl's other brother, Cleve, after several seasons in the professional North American Soccer League, came to Houston to work as a financial analyst for Dun and Bradstreet.

THE TELLEZ SYSTEM

Coach Tellez learned right away that Carl's right knee hurt and puffed up after a jump. An examination of Carl's legs showed that the left leg, called into service so often by Carl to take the place of the aching right, was actually thicker than the right. "I don't know how you jumped at all," Tellez told Carl.

Needed, said Tellez, was a program of therapy and exercise to build up the right leg so it would be the stronger leg. That was the good news. The bad news was that Carl would have to change the way he had been jumping. "As it was," Tellez said later, "the [knee] joint was taking all the strain that should have been absorbed by the muscular structure."

A NEW TECHNIQUE

Carl frowned. He didn't know if he could change. And should he change a style that had made him a high school champion? He told himself he would try. But during the next few months, using the new technique that Tellez was teaching him, Carl was landing in the sand only 22 or 23 feet from the takeoff line, not near the 26 feet, 8 inches he had jumped back in Willingboro.

A wave of panic swept over him as he got ready for a jump—"about 90 percent of the time," he said later. Tellez tried to calm him, saying he would never have exceeded 27 feet the way he had been jumping. But Carl wasn't even jumping 24 feet. Should he turn a deaf ear to this little man's ideas and go back to the way he had been jumping? Again the panic surged within him.

CHAPTER 3

DOUBLE TROUBLE

"Just look at our mother out there in the crowd," Carl shouted. "She's hugging and kissing and *everything!*"

It was a warm June afternoon in 1980. Evelyn Lewis was hugging and kissing friends and spectators in the stands in Eugene, Oregon. A few minutes earlier, seated with Bill and their three sons, she had watched her daughter Carol leap more than 20 feet to take third place in the long jump and do what she had sworn to do three years earlier—qualify for the 1980 U.S. Olympic team. Earlier in the meet Carl had also qualified for the team as a long jumper, finishing second to Larry Myricks, a husky jumper from Mississippi. Carl had missed qualifying for the 100 meters by a hair, finishing fourth. Both Carol and Carl already knew, however, that qualifying for the team was an honor that came with no ticket to Moscow: The U.S. team would not go to the Olympics because of President Jimmy Carter's outrage over the Soviet invasion of Afghanistan.

FRESHMAN YEAR

The winter and spring of 1979 and 1980, his freshman year at Houston, had been uphill months for Carl. The exercises and therapy had slowly taken effect. His right leg was now thicker than his left, which he no longer used to take off. Piece by piece, he was putting together what Tom Tellez called "the puzzle"—the step-by-step pieces of jumping technique which Tellez excelled at forging in the mind and body of a dutiful pupil. "The basic mechanics of long jumping have been around for years," Tellez said. "I know how to take those mechanics and put them into an athlete. And when you get an athlete like Carl, hey, that's what you dream about."

Tellez preached two basic principles. One was that getting up to top velocity during the approach to the takeoff bar and not losing that velocity at takeoff is the most important element of a long flight. As a sprinter with world-class speed, Carl had thought he needed only a run of about 140 feet to reach top speed at takeoff. To gain more speed, he had hurried through his last four eight-foot strides, his right foot staying on the takeoff bar a split-second too long during lift-off, which strained an already-sore patella tendon. At Tellez's direction, Carl had moved back to take a 147½-foot, 21-step approach. From this distance he was reaching the takeoff bar, without any awkward last-second rush, at close to 25 miles an hour. (Today Carl uses an even longer—171 feet, 23-step—approach to takeoff.)

"ATTACK THE AIR"

Secondly, Tellez insisted that while a lofty leap was dramatic, "you don't go anywhere that counts." He told Carl: "You're taking away the most important thing—that is, horizontal velocity—when you go upward instead of forward." In high school Carl had tried to hang high as long as he could, like a gull floating above the sand. Tellez taught him to drive through the leap like a baseball player jamming for a slide into second base. To get that drive, Tellez taught Carl to "attack the air," the arms windmilling, the legs scissoring and pedaling in what is called a "double-hitch kick."

Racing at 25 miles an hour at lift-off, Tellez concluded, could result in a crash landing, one potentially perilous to a jumper's neck. "With that speed at takeoff," he said, "the body tends to get overrotated. You don't want to do a somersault, so you have to create movement in the air to counteract it, and get your legs in good landing position.

A fear of flying makes some jumpers hesitant at takeoff. The sensation when a jumper leaps at top speed, Tellez said, is "scary and not a fun feeling." Some jumpers brake just before takeoff, scrubbing off much of that scary speed—what Carl disgustedly calls "backing down." Other jumpers don't like to leap when spectators crowd around the sand pit. As he gazes down upon the heads rushing up toward him, a jumper can experience the unnerving sensation that he might crash onto the roof of someone's skull.

Victory! Wearing his second 1984 Olympic gold medal and raising his winner's flowers, Carl waves to the cheering crowds. He won the medal with a long jump of 28 feet, ¼ inch.

The Lewis home in Willingboro, New Jersey. On this lawn Carl and Carol staged their "track meets."

Carl and his parents talk during a get-together in New York. Carl, at 6′2″, obviously got his height from both mother and father.

Carl and Carol pose at the place where their competitive careers began—near the sandpits of Willingboro High.

At the Willingboro High track where he ran his first scholastic races, Carl and a friend give some tips to youngsters on how to start.

In Rome in 1981 Carl sprays sand in winning the long jump at World Cup Games.

Carl takes the final approach step into a long jump of 28 feet, 3 inches at the UCLA-Pepsi Invitational Track Meet in Los Angeles in 1982. The leap set meet and stadium records.

At the 1982 UCLA-Pepsi Invitational, Carl shows his lift-off and the shift into the double-hitch kick at the midpoint of his long-jumping journeys through the air.

Carl soars toward the sandpit at the 1982 UCLA Pepsi meet. Note the straining upper-arm muscles as he fights to land cleanly with his weight pitching forward.

At an indoor meet in Dallas in February of 1983, Carl crosses the finish line first in the 60-yard dash, setting a new world indoor record of 6.02 seconds, breaking the old record of 6.82. Note how far in front he is in this race—the shortest of the races most sprinters run.

Off to his usual slow start at a 1983 Penn Relays race in Philadelphia, Carl (*third from left*) caught up with the leaders to win the 100 meters in 10:09, a meet record.

Arms held high in a victory gesture that probably cost him a world record, Carl crosses the line far ahead of everyone else to win the 200-meter race at the USA/Outdoor Championships at Indianapolis in 1983.

At Indianapolis in 1983, Carl qualifies for the trip to Helsinki and the World Championships by driving through the air and crashing into the sandpit for the second longest jump up to then—28 feet, 10¼ inches. Note how closely his form resembles a baseball player sliding toward a base.

At Helsinki for the 1983 World Championships, Carl gives a fan an autograph.

The winning quartet waves to the crowd after setting a new world record in the 400-meter relay event at Helsinki in 1983. The four are, (*left to right*) Emmit King, Carl, Willie Gault, and Calvin Smith.

At Helsinki in 1983, Carl (*left*) takes the baton from teammate Calvin Smith (*right*) for the anchor leg of the 400-meter relay. Carl beat Italy's Pietro Mennea to the finish line as the U.S. team set a world record.

At Helsinki, the three top finishers in the 100-meter dash pose with the flowers they were given before the medal presentation. Left to right, the top three are Calvin Smith, Carl, and Emmit King.

Carl holds the trophy presented to him early in 1984 for being named Gordon Gin's Black Athlete of the Year for 1983. In the voting, he beat out golf's Calvin Peete, basketball's Moses Malone, and football's Eric Dickerson.

At the U.S. Olympics Invitational meet in the New Jersey Meadowlands Arena in February 1984, Carl displays the same fine form that enabled him to set a world indoor long jump record of 28 feet, 10¼ inches the month before.

Running to glory. Carl heads for the 100-meter finish line and his first Olympic gold medal.

THE BIG JUMP

Carl's major problem was smoothing out the last four strides of his approach and mastering the flailing double-hitching flight. While still working out the kinks, however, freshman Carl managed to win the 1980 National Collegiate Athletic Association's indoor long-jumping championship. At times he soared over 26½ feet, but he wanted to make what he and Tellez called "the big jump"—to break the 27-foot barrier. Finally, in June of his freshman year, 1980, he sailed 27 feet, 4¾ inches to win the NCAA outdoor championship.

That leap was the third longest in long jump history—behind Beamon's 29 feet, 2½ inches and Larry Myricks's "sea-level" record of 27 feet, 11½ inches. But Carl's jump was not destined to make the record book; it had been pushed by a tail wind stronger than the legal limit of 2 meters a second.

Larry Myricks's so-called "sea-level" jump was considered by some to be the true world's record because Beamon's 29 foot-2½ inch-jump had been made in mountainous Mexico City. The "thin air" of Mexico City's high altitude, some experts maintained, made the Beamon leap a fluke that would never be equaled. (And, indeed, neither Beamon nor anyone else has ever again come close.)

As a 10-year-old boy Carl had put out that peg in his backyard and marveled at Beamon's prodigious accomplishment. As an 18-year-old freshman, he still wasn't sure it could be done. When reporters asked him if he thought the record could be broken, Carl often gave the answer Tellez gave: "We know 28 feet is just a matter of time. But 29? That's another matter. You can't predict that. No one can. All you can say is that it isn't inconceivable."

100-METER CHAMP

As a freshman Carl soon became the fastest on the team at 100 meters. His best time was 10.21 seconds, only 26 hundredths of a second off the existing world record of 9.95. Not so strangely, perhaps, that 9.95 record had been set by America's Jim Hines during the 1968 Olympics in the "thin-air" stadium at Mexico City.

By 1981, now a sophomore at Houston,

Carl was ranked the world's seventh best at 100 meters and the world's sixth best in the long jump. In both events he was chasing the ghosts of men who had set records they might not have set anywhere else in the world but Mexico City.

NEW INDOOR RECORD

At an indoor meet in Fort Worth early in 1981, Carl pounded down the boardwalk, each stride swallowing some 8 feet of board. His 21 strides took just 5 or 6 seconds—but there was so much to think about during the run that to Carl the dash seemed almost endless. What his thoughts were fixed on was ending the run with his right foot squarely on the ribbonlike takeoff bar—and not a smidgen beyond it. On the other side of the bar was a puttylike substance, Plasticene; the slightest touch by the toe of a shoe would leave an imprint on the Plasticene, indicating a foul that would nullify the jump.

Once his foot hit the takeoff bar, however, both Carl and time flew. "It's so quick you can't remember it," he said, "especially given how much we do in that amount of time—1.4 seconds is too fast for the mind to think and recapture it."

During that 1.4 seconds of flight at Fort Worth, Carl was windmilling his arms, scissoring and pedaling his legs, now the master of that double-hitching drive. As he landed, Carl heard the arena's silence split by a sought-after sound, the low and rising ooohing that builds swiftly to a thunderclap as the crowd sees that something extraordinary has occurred. On that day in 1981 Carl had soared farther than any man had ever before jumped in an indoor arena. The flight of 27 feet, 10¼ inches was Carl's first world record. Now he stood less than a foot and a half from Beamon's phenomenon.

Later in 1981, Carl ran 100 meters in 10 seconds flat, only five-hundredths of a second off Jim Hines's 9.95 that had stood for 13 years. In that meet Carl also won the 200-meter dash and anchored the 400-meter Houston relay team to a second-place finish. To conserve his energy, he took only one long jump, but that was good enough for 27 feet, ¾ inches, a Southwestern Conference record. Carl had scored 32 of his team's total 85 points.

NATIONAL RECOGNITION

By now he was recognized by track-and-field writers as one of the world's most versatile athletes. Said *The New York Times*: "Carl may be the only athlete who can run with Stanley Floyd, the world's top-rated sprinter, and jump in a class with East Germany's Luiz Dombrowski and Larry Myricks of the U.S."

Carl, too, considered himself more than a long-jumper. "I'm a jumper and a sprinter both," he said in 1981. "I'm tired of hearing people say I run to help my long-jumping. For the first time I'm training for both."

"I don't know what Carl's best event is," Tom Tellez said that spring. "He hasn't even tried what may have been his best event—the hurdles. With his speed and leaping ability he could be the greatest hurdler ever. I have never seen anyone like him."

COMPARISONS WITH JESSE OWENS

Inevitably, comparisons arise between Lewis and Jesse Owens, an athlete whose versatility hasn't been matched since his four gold medals in 1936. "I saw Jesse Owens and I saw Carl Lewis," said former University of Pennsylvania track coach Jim Tuppeny. "In my opinion Carl Lewis is a better athlete than Jesse Owens was."

There is a tremendous urge on the part of sportswriters to create Carl Lewis in the image of Jesse Owens. This seems unfair to both athletes. Times and track styles have changed dramatically. But Carl has adopted at least one winning technique from Owens. While most sprinters run with their hands balled up in fists, Lewis runs with his hands open like a cadet on parade maneuvers. The idea is that the balled-up fist creates a certain muscle tension which works against the runner's forward motion. Carl's open-handed style was taught to him by his father. Bill Lewis in turn adopted the technique from Jesse Owens. "I learned that one from the master," Bill Lewis told the *Daily News*.

TAKING RISKS

Carl knew that training for both running and jumping could be risky to his health and

told Tellez before the long-jumping qualifying began. He wanted to conserve his strength for the two 100-meter heats, the semi-final and the final. Carl fouled his first qualifying jump. On his next run he saw, as he approached the bar, that he would overstep and foul again. He took four choppy steps and took off, retaining so much velocity that when he came down, he had traveled 28 feet, 7 inches—at that time the second longest leap ever and only about a half-foot short of Beamon's record. But a look by the officials at the wind gauges showed a tailwind of 5 meters a second, 3 meters stronger than the legal limit. The leap wouldn't go into the records, but it did qualify him for the final. The next day, the stadium still seared with heat, Carl qualified for the 100 with a second-place finish of 10.25 seconds.

"MAKE THE FIRST ONE COUNT"

Carl walked to the runway for the long-jump final. He decided that he would take only one leap and hope it could stand off the best by Myricks. "Make the first one count," he told himself. He sprinted down the runway and saw he was a half-foot too close to the fouling point as he began his last two strides. Hastily he shifted to a shorter stride and sailed off toward the pit. He crashed heels first, sand spraying his face and chest, arms close to his hips, hands perilously close to his spiked shoes. Then he was pitching forward, rocking from a seated position as he catapulted out of the sand.

The crowd's roar broke above him. People were already on their feet, sensing that here was history being made. They had witnessed the second longest jump in history and the longest jump ever at sea level—28 feet, 3½ inches. There was no wind. Carl had come within a foot of one of his two ghosts.

Carl smiled and waved to the crowd, but within minutes his mind had turned to the 100, the last event of the four that would complete his double-double. He laced on his sprinting shoes to warm up for the 100, resisting the urge to try another jump until he saw what Myricks would do. If Larry flew beyond that 28 feet, 3½ inches, then Carl would have to come back after the "century" to try again.

COMING FROM BEHIND

Minutes later he crouched on the line for the start of the 100, Floyd and Lattany in the blocks near him. The starter's pistol snapped in the hot air. As usual, Carl came out of the blocks behind most everyone; the leader of the curving eight-man wave was at least an arm's length in front of him and swiftly pulling away. Carl, coming up from his starting crouch, did not press or break from his smoothly accelerating rhythm. At 30 meters he began to close on the front edge of the multi-colored wave. "I knew then," he said later, "that I had it." At 50 meters he was third. At 70 he was second. At 80 he pulled ahead. At 90 he glanced left and right at his trailing rivals and thrust up his arms, a happy signal of victory. Carl had begun to let all of his inner exultation rush out of him as he came to the finish line, looking back at beaten rivals and waving his hands as he seemingly tried to reach out and touch the roaring of the crowd.

Carl had won the 100 and, minutes later, he had won the long jump too, Myricks having fallen five inches short of Carl's single jump. Lewis had captured the double-double. "People said I couldn't do it," he said happily, "but I proved I could do it." Reporters dubbed him Double Trouble. But Double Trouble had some track people wondering. First of all, how could he ever be a world-class sprinter when he started so slowly? Second, if Carl Lewis was a better athlete than Jesse Owens who had won the 100 *and* 200 *and* the long jump in Berlin, then how come Carl Lewis had yet to win a major 200?

CHAPTER 4

"WHAT I REALLY WANT. . ."

"Ohhh, I'm having a *bad* day today," Carl muttered, shaking his head. He wiggled his long arms to relax them. He walked back onto the runway. Lewis was competing in a UCLA meet in Los Angeles on a warm spring day in 1982. On his first leap he had fouled and there were those watching him who wondered whether Carl and Coach Tellez had tinkered once too often with the jumper's approach.

A NEW APPROACH

Until now he had been running 147½ feet, or 21 strides, from the head of the runway to the takeoff board. But Carl was now so fast he was rated as the world's fastest at 100 meters. Carl and his coach dedided to add another 20 feet—and two more strides—to the approach run, figuring that that would boost velocity at takeoff.

Trouble was, he was going so fast that he had trouble controlling his last two strides. Too often he overstepped the takeoff board and fouled. Poised now at the top of the runway, the crowd silent, he put his left foot slightly forward. He stared intently toward the pit, a sandy thumb print in the distance. He shifted the weight to his right leg, made one goose-stepping stride forward, and took off. Lewis's drive for acceleration was formidable. As he took his 23rd and final stride, he was moving at 27 miles an hour. Up in the air, arms flailing and legs driving, he soared toward the pit and the photographers massed around its edges, cameras clicking, lights flashing. Of the leap, he once said, "It's so quick and comfortable that sometimes when I get out of the pit, I have to ask coach Tellez if I did all right."

He had done just fine here at UCLA, leaping 28 feet, 3 inches, the third longest jump in history and only a half-inch behind the second best—his 28 feet, 3½ inches that had won outdoors a year earlier. As Carl trotted toward Tellez, both were smiling. Another risky change in technique had paid off.

A GOOD YEAR

So far 1982 had been a bell-ringer for Carl. It started when he received the Sullivan Award, presented annually to the nation's outstanding amateur athlete. Then, at the U.S. Olympics Invitational at New Jersey's Meadowlands Arena he had soared 28 feet, 1 inch, to set a new world indoor record, breaking his own previous record of 27 feet, 10¼ inches set just a year earlier. Indeed, as Tellez and Lewis had predicted a year ago, the 28s would come. It was the 29s that were still in doubt.

In some minds that is. Not in Carl's. By the spring of 1982 he was predicting that Beamon's record would fall. "Boom! It will go," he told one reporter. And to *Sport* magazine's Mitch Albom, he said, "If men set those records, then another man can break them. Forget about the altitude at Mexico City. I believe I can get both records at sea level" (Beamon's 29′ 2½″ and Myrick's 27′11½″). Carl smiled. "And then," he said, "I'm gonna set some of my own."

THE SANTA MONICA TRACK CLUB

By now Carl had decided to quit the University of Houston track team. Early in 1982 he had failed a history course, making him ineligible to compete in college events because of NCAA rules on scholarship performance for athletes. He still had a passing average of about 3.0, and he could have made up the course, but Carl decided he had a responsibility to the Cougars to race in dual meets and pile up a lot of team points. On the other hand, he had a responsibility to himself and to what he called his "God-given gifts" to set new records in the 100 and the long jump. Carl felt that he couldn't pour all that energy into college meets and have enough left over to crack two world records.

Carl continued to attend classes at Houston, now a junior. He paid his own tuition. He joined the Santa Monica Track Club, whose coach was Joe Douglas, a man Carl and the Lewis family had come to know and trust. But Carl still worked out at Houston's Robertson Stadium with the Cougar track team. And his coach was still the soft-spoken Tom Tellez.

That spring in 1982, Double Trouble again proved worthy of his nickname, winning both the long jump and the 100 meters at the U.S.A. Outdoor Nationals. He won the 100 meters in 10.11 seconds, the long jump at 27 feet, 10 inches. Not even Jesse Owens had won both events in a national meet two years in a row, a "double-double," proclaimed *Sports Illustrated*, "unique in this century."

THE "OTHER LEWIS"

The Houston Cougar team had lost one Lewis sibling, but it had gained another. Carol Lewis was now a freshman at her brother's school. At Willingboro she had been leaping more than 21 feet, longer than almost any high school girl, and here at the

Nationals she soared 22 feet, 4½ inches, the second longest jump ever by an American woman (The record was 22 feet, 11¾ inches.) Whatever Carl could do against male competitors, Carol maintained, she could do in female competition. And while Carol didn't want to make any big deal about it, she let it be known in a quiet way that she had grown tired of being referred to as "Carl Lewis's sister."

FAME AND FORTUNE

In the summer of 1982, Carl turned down invitations to tour Europe with other athletes, opting to stay closer to home. That option was costly to Carl, who was receiving offers as large as a reported $3,500 to compete in European meets. New U.S. amateur rules freed up athletes to receive money for meets and for promoting products in magazine ads and TV commercials. The money had to be put into a trust fund from which the athletes could draw out funds for "expenses." But as one athlete put it, "the word 'expenses' covers just about anything you can think of." Carl was now driving a shiny black Audi and living with Mackie in an apartment in Houston, which was decorated with expensive furniture and all the other creature comforts. Carl was fast becoming not just a sports celebrity but a national idol.

BEYOND BEAMON'S MARK

Running that summer of '82 in U.S. meets, Carl unreeled a 10-second-flat 100-meter, his fastest ever. He went to Indianapolis for the National Sports Festival. He took off on a leap estimated by some spectators to have been over 30 feet. But an official ruled he had fouled. Before the jump could be measured, Carl's mark was raked from the sand. Carl seldom complained about a foul call but this time he lodged a protest, asking the official to show him just where his foot had scuffed the Plasticene surface beyond the takeoff bar, the telltale marks of a foul. No one could find the marks. Still the leap did not count. Carl always believed that on that day in Indianapolis he had gone beyond Beamon's 29-footer. On his next leap he achieved 28 feet, 9 inches, the longest officially recognized jump ever, and the second longest of all time. He had now broken Myrick's record and come within six inches of Beamon's 29 feet, 2½ inches, the jump he had once considered as impossible as leaping the Grand Canyon, and within five-hundredths of a second of Jim Hines's 9.95.

"BOOM—I'M GONE!"

His sprinting coach at Houston told him he would easily make up that five-hundredths of a second with a quicker start out of the blocks. Carl, thinking independently more and more, wasn't so sure.

"A human being can only accelerate for 60 meters straight out," he once said. "The rest is just hanging on. So I start my acceleration a little faster and spread it out more. Look, I may get out of the blocks late, but when the other guys are reaching their max around 50 meters, I'm still building up my speed. By 70 meters I've caught them. They're slowing down as I hit my peak. And then—boom!—I'm gone."

To another writer he put it this way: "The

race is basically two elements: the acceleration and the relaxation periods. Acceleration starts when they shoot the gun. People criticize me for being a poor starter, but the start is only the beginning of the acceleration period. I'm always in control, or right at the front, by 40 or 50 or 60 meters. That's where my acceleration is at its peak. Everyone in the race starts to decelerate from 50 to 70 meters and continues to the tape. You cannot run full speed for 100 meters. The human body can only run full speed for 10 or 15 meters at a time. At 50 meters I often make a major move and really zoom by them. I've been able to master the deceleration or relaxation period so I can stay closer to full speed from 70 meters to the tape than anybody in the world."

THE BEST EVER

Later in 1982, Carl said, "Sometimes I look out the window and I say to myself, 'You know you can run and jump better than anyone else out there . . . But then I realize that it's all just for now. What I really want is to be the best ever." And he added to someone else:

"The only thing I am afraid of is that I'm not going to be the perfect athlete some day."

An important arena would be Los Angeles in 1984. But he also had a chance to prove he was the best now as 1983 came closer—at Indianapolis against the best of the United States and in Helsinki against the best of the world.

CHAPTER 5

LIKE O.J., AN ACTOR?

A WORLD RECORD—ALMOST

At 50 meters Carl surged even with the wavy line of runners, the shimmering reds, yellows, and blues of their track suits an undulating rainbow. At 60 meters he inched ahead. And as Carl leaned into the finish line, the crowd, seeing the wide gap between him and the other sprinters, let out a roar. Carl looked toward the electronic clock at Mount San Antonio College in Walnut, California, on this April day in 1983. He smiled. He saw a time of 9.93 seconds, two-hundredths of a second under Jim Hines's 100-meter record. At sea level or on top of a mountain, Carl Lewis finally owned a world record.

But officials immediately brought him back to earth. The tailwind had been measured at 2.30 meters per second, three tiny tenths of a meter too strong a push for the time to go into the record book. Once more a world record had been plucked from Carl's outstretched hands.

SPREADING HIMSELF THIN

Carl went back to Houston to train for the 1983 National Track and Field championship at Indianapolis. By finishing first, second, or third, he would qualify to compete against the world's best at Helsinki later in the summer in three events—the 100, the 200, and the long jump. For the past two years Carl had been told he was foolish to dilute his time and talent by spreading himself too thin, competing in both the 100 and the long jump. Now he was spreading himself thinner still with the addition of the 200-meter. The 200-meter is an interesting race, run on a curve. Carl looked forward to the opportunity to prove himself against world-class sprinters in that distance.

THE GOOD LIFE

Carl was a very rich sprinter. Because of those new amateur rules, he was earning fees estimated by reporters to be anywhere from $100,000 to $250,000 a year. Meet promoters were said to be offering him as much as $4,500 an appearance. He made TV commercials for Nike, the running-shoe people, and Fuji Xerox, the Japanese maker of office copiers.

Joe Douglas, the Santa Monica Track Club coach, was his full-time business manager. "He's not hurting for money," Douglas once said. And he added: "A lot of people look at Carl Lewis and they see dollar signs."

But wasn't Carl an amateur?

Douglas pointed to other track stars like Edwin Moses and Mary Decker, both said to be earning at least as much as Carl, and said, "It's a scam to say anybody's an amateur."

Carl's new white BMW carried this bit of philosophy on its license-plate frame: There

Is No Finish Line. He had moved out of his apartment and was living in a towering bay-windowed Victorian mansion in Houston. A uniformed servant greeted visitors. A visitor from *Newsweek* magazine saw a table set with Baccarat crystal and Christofle silver. An Oriental rug and Provençal furniture graced the living room. Many of the furnishings had been picked up in Europe by Carl, who was developing a connoisseur's eye. Carl once pointed out to a reporter with the rapt enthusiasm of a true collector how the colors of the Oriental rug seemed to shift and change as sunlight flooded through the mansion's French doors.

Attired in a blue silk Japanese bathrobe embroidered with the figure of a golden serpent, Carl told the *Newsweek* reporter: "I do like to spend money. But I only like to have things I can take pride in." A careful and conservative dresser, he had closets full of new suits, jackets, and slacks, and a half dozen brightly colored velour jogging suits. *Life* magazine photographed him in a wide-brimmed Safari-type hat and a banker's dark gray pin-striped suit. At the wheel of one of his glistening sports cars, Carl looked like a young Hollywood movie producer.

THE FAST LANE

Yet he confessed to listeners that he wasn't always the easy rider in the fast lane nor the calm man at the controls of his life. "I am only comfortable," he once said, "when I run or when I sleep. The rest of the time I just complain." He was so jumpy, he once said, that he would rarely sit still for a game of cards, a favorite time-killer among athletes. The chancy nature of card games, he said, made him more nervous than he had ever been before a big race.

Now a senior, he was still majoring in broadcasting and the communication arts at Houston. He gave much serious thought to what direction his career might take after he crossed his last finish line. He thought, he said, that he would compete for only a year or two after the 1984 Olympics. Pro football teams had talked about drafting him for his speed. (The Dallas Cowboys later did.) Pro basketball teams talked about drafting him for his leaping. (The Chicago Bulls later did.) Carl was interested in less violent careers. "I'd like to go into broadcasting in radio and television," he said. "But I'm also thinking about doing public relations work. I can't stay in one event in track and field so I know I couldn't stay in one career."

Young ladies were a fixture in Carl's world. Sister Carol sometimes teased women athletes that they had their sights set on her brother, an allegation infrequently denied. "I do go to dinner with girl friends or whatever," Carl told *Newsweek*'s reporter, "and interact. But basically I travel so much and I'm so involved right now that it's difficult to channel my mind into other avenues. I want to go in stages—track, then another career, then marriage and a family."

Questioners, as they will with celebrities, frequently asked him about his sex life. "As for sex," he would tell an interviewer from *Gentlemen's Quarterly*, "well, it's different strokes for different folks. I shouldn't say this, but I've done something the night before a meet, and I did horribly and done something the night before and set a record. But I'll have my parents at the Olympics. I won't have a choice."

He had twice been asked to pose in the nude. "One was *Playgirl* magazine," he said. "The other was Annie Liebowitz for *Vanity Fair*. I turned them both down."

THE TRIPLE: TAKING THE RISK

Early in June he arrived at Indianapolis for the Athletic Congress's National Track and Field Championship. Carl and Tellez debated whether he should try for a triple here at Indianapolis, victories in the 100, 200, and the long jump. A first, second, or third in the 100 meters would qualify him for a leg on the 400-meter relay team at the World Championships in Helsinki later in the summer. Helsinki, then, could be a practice run for what he was now aiming for at Los Angeles in 1984—the winning of four gold medals.

"You are going out on a limb," Tellez told Carl, who still listened closely to his coach but who was now making the final decisions himself. They talked of the dangers to a sprinter, tired after a couple of 100 meters, in attempting the long jump. "The forces necessary to hurl a 175-pound man nearly 30 feet through the air are more than enough to snap ankle bones," pointed out former runner Kenny Moore in *Sports Illustrated*. "A tired jumper must accept an increase in that risk."

Carl decided to take the risk. He won his

100-meter heat and the semi-final. Then, with a wind in his face, he ran the final to win in 10.27 seconds. He won the long jump with a leap of 28 feet, 10¼ inches, his best ever, putting him within five inches of Beamon's record. And in the finals of the 200, against world-class competition for the first time, he ran away from the field, thrusting his hands high in triumph some 5 meters from the finish line. His time was 19.75 seconds, only three-hundredths of a second off the world record of 19.72. If he had not raised his hands, he would certainly have owned his first world outdoor record. He had accomplished the triple at the Nationals at Indianapolis, something no one had done in American track and field in 97 years. He had come within a whisker of setting a world record in a race for which he had only recently begun to train.

BACKLASH

Yet Carl heard murmers of disapproval mingled with the cheers. Fellow athletes growled that Carl had become a show-off, looking around at his trailing rivals as he approached the finish line, thrusting up his hands in a V-shaped sign of victory. They chided him publicly for failing to set a record in the 200 because he had chosen instead to "showboat." Hurdler Edwin Moses said, "I've talked to a lot of people and the words they used were 'lack of sportsmanship.' Everybody knows he's a big winner and nobody envies him or anything like that. But for some people it's a little too much." And, he added, of Carl's propensity for looking back at his rivals and throwing up his hands, "I think he rubs it in too much. There's a lot of negative vibrations about the guy."

His No. 1 rival in the long jump, Larry Myricks, who had owned the U.S. long-jumping title before Carl said softly: "There's going to be some celebration when Carl gets beaten. And I know he can be beaten."

CARL SPEAKS OUT

Carl defended himself. He was not showboating, he insisted, he was simply being himself. "It's emotion. It's me. I was that way when I was six years old. I don't mind that other people don't show emotions like I do. But I do mind when they say I shouldn't.

Men athletes especially have to be like King Kong. When we lose we can't cry. And we can't pout. We're not supposed to be touched [by emotions]. We have to be carved in a certain way, to be men"—he tapped his chest with his knuckles—"chests of steel and all. I think it's disgusting."

Later he would say to a *Time* reporter: "People are trying to say I'm two different personalities, that I wear two masks. Outside the house, friendly and happy. Inside cold, calculating, even evil. Sometimes I find this world baffling."

To someone else he said, "I get fun and joy from track. Raising my arms when I win is the only means of expression I have. It's also one way you can relax in a race. Maybe if I had kept driving toward the finish (in the 200 meters) I might have hurt myself."

People in track and field who had known Carl since he was in high school insisted that he acted toward others as he always had. "He's always said hello as long as I've known him," said New York City track coach Fred Thompson. "Even today, when I saw him, I said congratulations. And he said, 'Hey, thanks a lot.' What I'm saying is that he's never been on a head trip."

CELEBRITY STATUS

Carl later acknowledged the criticism. "One thing that gets people talking," he once told an interviewer from *Gentlemen's Quarterly*, "is that when I go to track meets, I like to stay in my room, maybe have dinner with my family, and then go to sleep. I'm not in the lobby with the athletes; I'm not playing cards with them. I don't interact as much, so everyone thinks I'm uppity or stuck up . . ."

Inevitably, however, Carl has been somewhat altered by all the attention and adulation. He wears a celebrity's huge dark glasses as he pushes through mobs of well wishers upon leaving a stadium to get to his car. He wears tight, colorful warm-up suits. He tosses toothy-white smiles at TV cameras and photographers. He weaves his way through shrieking autograph seekers. He accepts the frenzy that often swirls around him when he appears in public, but he wants to keep a shield between it and himself. "I can't get into that part of it or I'd go crazy," he told *The New York Times* writer Jane Gross. "Carol likes it. I tolerate it. I like the quiet part of it, when I'm on the track. That's still sacred to me—the competition and the fun of it."

A NEW ROLE MODEL

He had also changed his role model by 1983. Now he hardly ever referred to himself as another Jesse Owens. He was talking and living a life style more like O.J. Simpson, the ex-football player turned actor and TV personality. Like O.J., Carl began to see himself as more than a TV broadcaster.

As part of his Houston studies, Carl went to New York to take acting lessons. "The first day," he later told Jane Gross, "the teacher told me that athletes make horrendous actors because we're trained to suppress our emotions." He grinned. "Well, I was good, I was really good."

His teacher did not dispute Carl's rave review of himself. The teacher, Warren Robertson, told an interviewer: "He may seem cool and impersonal at first, but I think that's because he is fundamentally shy and doesn't want to waste his energy on something or somebody unless he feels its really worthwhile. In that sense he's very self-contained. We only worked together for about a month, but even in that time he showed exceptional promise. For a workshop class we did some scenes from the television movie *Brian's*

Song, in which Carl played the football hero Gale Sayers. He was astonishingly good in rehearsal, but even better when performing in front of a class. He seemed to know intuitively how to focus on the essentials."

FOUR IN HELSINKI?

Late in July of 1983, however, Carl's primary attention was fixed on Helsinki, where he had a chance to compete in the 100, the 200, the long jump and the 400-meter relay, the four events he hoped to win at Los Angeles in the 1984 Olympics.

Should he go for four in Helsinki?

Carl pondered the question. There were good reasons to say yes, good reasons to say no.

CHAPTER 6

"CAROL LEWIS'S BROTHER"

Six-foot-3-inch, 175-pound Carl Lewis stood on the track at the Helsinki stadium, the place where his mother had wanted so much to be thirty-one years before. She would have been chilly here, Carl thought to himself. Though he was wearing an electric-blue velour running suit, Carl shivered as a cool, damp wind blew across the infield.

THE 200: IS IT WORTH IT?

Standing with Carl was Tom Tellez. The coach was making a case against Carl's running the 200 meters here, arguing that Carl should restrict himself to three events—the 100, the 4 × 100-meter relay, and the long jump. On a cool day a tired athlete was more likely to snap something, Tellez said. Carl could be laid up for months. An injury here could mean that he would go to Los Angeles for the Olympics weeks or months behind in his training schedule. For days Carl weighed what he should do. He had been doing a lot of thinking lately about the 200-meter race, a tricky one, more technical than the 100. You ran the 100 straight ahead to a finish line like the Oklahoma stampede. The 200 required a little more strategy and tactics. The real race often started near the top of the backstretch.

On a curved track the starting lines are staggered by lane. Each runner starts about a meter ahead of the runner on his left. Staggered starting blocks compensate for the difference in distances run by inside and outside runners on the oval. Those on the inside have less ground to cover around the curve than those in the outside lanes. To make up the difference, runners in the inside lanes start a few meters farther from the finish line than those in the outside lanes. For runners and spectators alike it is difficult to tell—because of the staggered start—who is ahead during the race around the curve. But as the runners come out of the turn into the straightaway, it quickly becomes clear who is leading. For a slow starter like Carl the collaring of the leaders might be especially difficult if he didn't know who was ahead in the curve. Moreover, 200-meter runners have to learn how to tilt their bodies for maximum speed as they round a curve. For all of his life Carl had run straight up. Tilt too little, he had learned, and you go too slow. Tilt too much, he had also discovered, and you wobble.

Yet Carl, practicing 200s, was beginning to admire the event. "I like the long jump the most by far," he told people. "Of course, I'm biased, but I think the long jump has the best athletes in the world." There was Jesse Owens, he pointed out, who had set a record in 1936 that stood for 24 years. And then there was Bob Beamon who has set a record still standing after fifteen years. "The long jump," Carl said, more than a little tongue in cheek, "has had people who moved ahead of their time."

But when he had to choose between the 100 and 200 as his second favorite, he was no longer sure. "In the past the 100 was my second favorite, but now it's becoming very close between the 100 and the 200. I will always like the 100 because the world champion at 100 meters is called the world's fastest human, and I have always wanted that title. The 200 is a lot tougher to run, but it's the more technical and I think that makes it more interesting and appealing to me."

A RECORD WITHIN HIS REACH

What also had to make the 200 more appealing to him was the fact that the world record of 19:73 seconds, set by Italy's Pietro Mennea, had not been set in the lessened air resistance of Mexico City. Compared to the "thin-air" records that Carl was chasing in the 100 and long jump, the "sea-level" record for the 200 seemed more quickly attainable. And Carl well knew that for all his accomplishments in sport, he was one of the few top stars in track and field who had never set an outdoor world record.

While in Europe for the World Championships in Helsinki, Carl and other U.S.

athletes competed in a meet at Malmo, Sweden. Carl chose the 200 and won with a good time of 20:27 seconds. That seemed an augur telling him to go for the 200 and four golds at Helsinki.

GOING FOR THREE GOLDS

But Tellez's concerns about an injury that could wreck his chances in '84 at Los Angeles finally convinced Carl. He said he would skip the 200 and try "only" for three golds at Helsinki.

His first event was the long jump. His first leap was 28 feet, ¾ inches, only so-so for Carl. But he figured no one else in the world could beat it. He passed up his remaining jumps to rest for the 100-meter heats. While he watched the other jumpers strain, in vain, to reach 28 feet, he gave tips to fellow Americans Jason Grimes and Mike Conley. They finished second and third behind Carl. It was the first sweep by the United States of an international long-jumping event since the 1904 Olympics.

Carl then won the 100-meter, the time 10.07 seconds in a race run against a stiff headwind. The American team—Carl, Calvin Smith, Emmit King and Willie Gault—qualified for the finals of the 400-meter relay.

Carl was running the anchor leg. Smith, running the third leg, handed him the baton and a one-yard lead ahead of Italy's Pietro Mennea, the 200-meter world record holder. Carl shot away from the Italian to win by five yards. At the finish, knowing he was running this race for three other guys and not only for himself, he did not throw up his arms. He dipped his body into the tape to get the fastest time and only as Gault ran toward him to embrace him did Carl throw up his arms in happiness. All four knew they had set a world record. The time was 37.86 seconds.

WORLD'S FASTEST MAN?

Officials later studied a videotape and discovered that Carl had run that last 100 meters, with a flying start, in 8.9 seconds (since it had been a flying start, it was not, of course, a world record.) "There is no evidence that any man has ever run faster," wrote Kenny Moore in *Sports Illustrated*. "So it is time that Lewis's sobriquet, 'the best American athlete since Jesse Owens,' be retired. Among sprinters and among jumpers he is the best, ever." One French sporting paper gave Carl a new name: Superman.

Superman stood in the infield to watch his sister, Carol, now twenty years old and soon to be a junior at Houston, compete in the long jump. She finished in third place with a leap of 23 feet, ¼ inch, the longest leap till then by an American woman. "Now," she said to her brother with an impish look, "maybe you're going to be Carol Lewis's brother."

ON THE SIDELINES

Carol Lewis's brother watched the runners line up for the final of the 200 meters. "It was not easy for me to watch the 200 at Helsinki," he later told an interviewer from *Runner's World* magazine. "There was a little bit inside of me that wanted to be out there."

America's Calvin Smith finished first. Would Carl have beaten Calvin in that 200 and come home with four pieces of gold? "When I compete against Calvin," Carl said,

"I'm extremely confident because I know I'm as talented as he is. . . . We're Christian friends first and athletic friends second. But the main advantage I have is experience. I feel I have been a little more consistent in some of the bigger meets. . ." Of the five 200 races in which Carl and Calvin had competed, Carl pointed out, he had won three.

Carl's religious beliefs are integrally linked with his athletics. He is an active member of an athletic evangelical association called the Lay Witnesses for Christ. When Carl speaks of his "God-given talent," he means it sincerely.

THE BUILDUP OF CARL LEWIS

Back in the United States, the countdown for the Olympics—less than ten months away—had begun. Of all the U.S. athletes likely to compete, Carl was the most sought after by reporters and TV crews who swarmed into Houston. Joe Douglas tried to steer his client into the pages of general interest magazines to increase public awareness of who he was and what he might do in 1984.

Articles on Carl increased in frequency and scope. The Carl Lewis buildup was on. He was seen and quoted in the pages of *Life, Newsweek, Esquire, The New York Times,* and *Gentlemen's Quarterly.*

Joe Douglas, meanwhile, talked of Carl signing contracts with one or two large corporations to serve as their spokesman as O.J. Simpson had done for General Motors and Hertz. "When Carl negotiates his contracts after the Olympics," he told Jane Gross of the *Times*, "he will be just as valuable as Michael Jackson. He won't be just a track or a sports star. He will be a personality."

Douglas talked of Michael Jackson's contract with Pepsi-Cola that was worth a reported $5.5 million and said, "That's my reference point."

But Lewis went on to say to *Time* reporters, "I can't sing as well as he does, and I don't think he can run as fast as I do, so I don't fear him, and there's no reason for him to fear me."

"When you have money, you have a lot of freedom," Lewis added. "It's no big deal, but I understand its value."

Carl can be a very funny man. A reporter once asked him about the Dallas Cowboys and the Chicago Bulls drafting him for football and basketball. The fact that Carl had never even played organized basketball didn't seem to faze pro clubs. "On days when I'm sitting and doing nothing," Carl announced deadpan, "I look in the paper to see who has drafted me."

GOALS FOR 1984

As 1984 began, Carl had long-jumped 28 feet or better thirteen times. He held the world indoor record of 28 feet, 1 inch. He had jumped farther outdoors, 28 feet, 10¼ inches, than anyone except Beamon. He had run the 100 in 9.97 seconds, faster than anyone except Hines, Calvin Smith, and Mel Lattany. He had run the 200 in 19.75 seconds, faster than any American. And he had been part of a 400-meter relay team that owned the world record.

He had yet to set an individual world outdoor record. "The records are in Carl Lewis," he said. "Getting them out is my responsibility. If I don't it will be a flat waste of a person."

He seemed determined to put more of a

burden on his shoulders to succeed than even the world was demanding. "I like to improve," he said, speaking of what he expected of himself in 1984. "I've improved every single year of my career, every single event. So it's scary. That's the one fear I have."

The fear of having to be better. . . *and* better. . . especially when you will be twenty-three in August of 1984 and competing in the only Olympics of your life, and you've told yourself and the world that if you don't become the best ever, maybe you wasted all that God-given talent.

"Wasting a gift is a terrible thing," he once said, "and I have always told myself to get the very most out of what God has given me. Nobody expects more from Carl Lewis than Carl Lewis."

CHAPTER 7

GOING FOR FOUR!

"THE BEST JUMP OF MY LIFE"

What a way to start an Olympic year. Carl Lewis stood grim-faced at the head of the runway in a packed Madison Square Garden in early February of 1984, looking down the board runway at the sandpit where photographers crouched like snipers. After thirty straight long-jump victories, Carl seemed headed for a defeat that would end the streak—an ugly omen of things to come in '84.

He was poised for his sixth and last jump at the 1984 Millrose Games. His old rival,

Larry Myricks, had jumped 27 feet, 6 inches, and Carl hadn't been able to better that effort. One trouble was a loose board on the runway and Carl had slipped on it.

His feisty sister, Carol, now the U.S. women's long-jumping champion, offered to hold the board. Now, seated on the Garden floor, she braced the board with her feet.

Down the runway Carl sped. His foot hit the takeoff board, his toe so close to the Plasticene foul strip that a judge later said he'd missed it by no more than the thickness of tissue paper. Carl soared like a madly flailing bird toward the pit, the Garden silent. When he hit, the sudden roar was like a dam breaking, the crowd seeing that he had sailed past Myricks's best. The only question was, how far past. The answer came quickly: Carl had achieved 28 feet, 10¼ inches, his longest jump indoors and tying his longest jump outdoors, accomplished at Indianapolis in '83. The next day track experts said that if Carl had made that approach and jump outdoors and there had been the slightest favoring wind, he would have bulleted at least 30 feet. "It was," said Carl, "the best jump of my life."

THE BEGINNING OF THE 1984 SEASON

When the 1984 outdoor season began, Carl worked hard during his Monday-to-Thursday work week on the 200. (He competed most Saturdays.) At one meet he ran a 20:01, the fourth fastest time ever. He had won the race, but when he finished there was a worried look on his usually smiling face. During the last 20 meters, Lee Evans had been gaining on Carl. In 100-meter races it was generally Carl who ran away from people in the last 20 meters. Here, in the 200, someone had been gaining on *him*. "It wasn't like winning at 100 meters," Carl said, shaken, "that's for sure."

Other runners thought Carl might be in for an unpleasant surprise when he tried to qualify for the U.S. team in the 200 at the Olympic trials to be held in Los Angeles in June. One sprinter, Steve Williams, said, "The 100 and the long jump combination is a mustering of force. The 200 is more of a sustained thing and even though Carl runs a good curve. . .he will find the 200 a little different."

THE OLYMPIC TRIALS

In June, 900 of America's best men and women track and field athletes came to the trials at Los Angeles Memorial Stadium, where the Olympics would take place six short weeks later. Many of the competitors held world and U.S. records. But records meant little in this trial by ordeal. Only the first three finishers in each event would make the U.S. team. Of the 900, as many as 800 would be watching the '84 Olympics from seats in the stadium or on TV at home. "Making the team is the big thing," said one competitor. "After this, the Olympics will be easy."

Aware that he was expected to win four events at these trials, Carl was nonetheless cool, poised and in control at press conferences. His acting lessons—and perhaps an appearance the ex-cello player had made conducting the Houston Symphony Orchestra in the music from "Chariots of Fire"—had given him even more of a stage presence. At one press conference a reporter asked if it was true that Carl made a million dollars a year. Smiling, Carl said he didn't think it was anybody's business how much other people earned. He asked the reporter: "How much do you make?"

"Thirty eight thousand a year."

"How many here make less than that?" Carl asked, laughing.

Among those who raised their hands was sister Carol, always one to get into an act. "No, Carol," Carl said firmly. "You don't make less than that."

GOING FOR FOUR

Tom Tellez studied Carl's schedule for the trials, which would be much the same schedule Carl would face at the Olympics in August. Carl had to run two 100-meter heats on a Saturday, the semi-finals and the finals on Sunday. On Monday he had to qualify for the long jump. On Tuesday he would face the long-jump final and two heats of the 200. On Thursday there would be the 200 semi-finals and the 200 final. One slight misstep, one bad start in any one of eight races, and Carl would be among the billions around the world looking at the 100, 200, or long jump instead of competing in them.

THE 100-METER

As the trials began, he seemed distracted, even tense. And forgetful. He went to the dressing room before the start of a 100-meter heat, then came back to the starting line and started to take off his jogging pants. He looked down and saw he had forgotten his shorts. Joe Douglas sprinted to the dressing room and rushed back to his client with a new pair. Carl hastily slipped them on in a room off the track.

He won that 100 heat. He won another, qualifying for the semi-finals the next day. An impish official handed out the results of the heats. For the heat Carl had won, he had written, "won by Carol Lewis's brother." He showed it to Carol who said, smiling, "Finally you guys have got it right."

By now Carol had twice been the national women's long-jumping champion. Her longest leap had been slightly more than 22 feet. In the trials she got a bad scare when she fouled on the first two of her three qualifying attempts. One her third and last try, she flew well past 21 feet to qualify. And an hour later she jumped 22 feet, 7¼ inches to finish first among the women and win herself a place on the U.S. Olympic team.

In the 100-meter men's final were the three men who had run the fastest 100s in the past 10 years: Carl (9:97), Mel Lattany (9:96) and Calvin Smith (9:93). A 5-mph wind whipped into their faces as the eight runners jammed the flat bottoms of their shoes against the starting blocks. The gun cracked. Carl broke late, almost seeming to stumble on his first few steps as he rose into sprinting position, the point of the snaky line perhaps half an arm's length ahead. At 30 meters he had accelerated close to maximum velocity and at 50 he forged into the lead. At 80 meters he glanced left and then right, saw he was ahead by at least a meter. As he approached the line, both hands thrust high, he was smiling, ahead by almost two meters. His time of 10:06 was fast considering the head wind, but most importantly, he had put himself on the U.S. Olympic team in two of the four events he wanted to be in—the 100 and the 4 × 100-meter relay.

THE LONG JUMP

The next day he qualified for the long jump with the day's best leap—27 feet, 6¼ inches, then won it the following day with 28 feet, 7 inches, a foot and a half longer than Larry Myricks's. Now he had the number 3 event and he was going for the number 4, the tricky 200 meters.

THE 200-METER

He won the two 200 heats. On Thursday afternoon, June 21, with ABC-TV cameras poking out of the stands to send the race live to an expectant America, Carl knelt into the starting blocks at the head of the stretch, arms straining against the salmon-pink artificial track surface. At the gun the eight runners bolted into the curve. Kirk Baptiste, the U.S. collegiate champion, seemed to have the lead, but when the ragged line came out of the curve into the straightaway, Carl had forged ahead. Runners were fading away from him as he beat Baptiste by two yards. His time, 19.86 seconds, was Carl's third best ever, but that was not uppermost in his mind as he bounded happily down the track. He told the nation what was first in his mind as he raised his right hand and showed four fingers.

Four! He had gone four! And he had made four!

"THE FIRST CARL LEWIS"

He fell to the ground on both knees and kissed the track, thanking God, he said later, for the gifts he had been given—and what he had done with those gifts. Could he win four golds at the Olympics and be the new Jesse Owens? "I want to be considered the first Carl Lewis," he said, repeating what he had said so often during the past two years. "The whole Jesse Owens thing is not dead, but I'm doing this because I think it's attainable for me." And he added, "I'm competing in the four events not because of Jesse but because of me and who I am."

Later he told a reporter: "I know what it takes to win. It takes, of course, hard work. It takes careful planning. It takes a spiritual life. It also takes simple relaxation. And right now I have all those elements so I am not afraid."

CHAPTER 8

A TIME FOR WAITING

Carl watched as Gina Hemphill, Jesse Owens's granddaughter, circled the track of the Los Angeles Coliseum, the oval infield a colorful patchwork of the blazing reds, purples, blues, and golds of the uniforms worn by some 10,000 athletes from 140 nations. To friends and family watching the Olympic opening ceremonies from their seats high above the Coliseum field, Carl and Carol were lost in that sea of dazzling color.

On this sunny July 28 in Los Angeles, a clear and warm day, the eyes of the 100,000 spectators in the Coliseum—and those of the millions watching on television sets around the world—were fixed on the white-shirted young runner as she circled the track, Olympic torch gripped in her right hand. Carl needed no more reminder of what was expected of him once the track and field competition began a week from now.

Indeed, *Time* magazine had already photographed him for the cover of its next issue, anticipating that he would win his first event, the 100 meters. *Time* had captioned the cover photo "One down! Three to go!"

OUT OF SECLUSION

By attending the opening ceremonies, Carl was making a rare public appearance. Some athletes had hinted that he might not even come. During the past two weeks, as U.S. and foreign athletes streamed into their quarters at the Olympic villages scattered around Los Angeles, Carl had hidden himself, with Carol and their mother and father, in a rented two-story stucco house on a quiet street, half a dozen miles from the Coliseum.

Carl told U.S. Olympic officials that he would not check into his room at one of the villages. The officials insisted that he must obey the rules like any other athlete. Joe Douglas and Carl argued that Carl was a "visible" athlete. Even if he only strolled through the Village, Carl said, he would be mobbed by reporters, camera crews, and fellow athletes seeking autographs. Carl said his training program and his concentration would be wrecked by all the attention. "The main issue," Carl told officials, "is for me to compete well, not to be sure every person stays here or there."

Carl finally agreed to check into an Olympic Village on the tightly guarded UCLA campus, but only briefly. Even during a short stay, Joe Douglas growled, "The first time it gets noisy, Carl will check out and stay at a private hotel."

In fact, Carl didn't stay long enough to hear any noise. He moved back to the rented house and trained at a secluded and guarded track in Santa Monica. There, on a warm morning in early August, Carl went through the last practice for the ultimate events of his competitive life—the 14 heats, semifinals, and finals he faced during the nine days from August 4th's first 100-meter heat until the final of the 400-meter relay on August 11th. There could be no slips, no stumbles. One bad start in a heat and he would be watching the finals of the event on television.

HE LIKED IT HOT

Hot California days suited him fine for training and competition. The hotter it was, he told people, the stronger and faster he felt. In any kind of weather, *Time* magazine reporter Melissa Ludtke observed, "Carl does everything slowly except run. He is slow to start his workout. His warm-up is usually a slow jog around the track. He spends a lot of time talking and walking slowly. . . . His final workout lasts 40 minutes. During that time he takes only three runs. He is in action for a scant total of 30 seconds."

Which was enough, believed Carl and Tellez. For some ten odd years Carl had built his body for these final minutes of Olympic jumping and running. The body was as strong and its engine as finely tuned as they could be. As Carl told Melissa Ludtke: "At the Olympics it is one hundred percent mental because there is nothing [more] you can do physically."

Back at the Lewis hideaway, Evelyn did the cooking for her husband and their two Olympians. Cooking helped keep her fidgety feelings under control as she awaited the second week of the Olympics, and the start of the track and field events for Carl and Carol. One of Carl's favorite dishes was Evelyn's version of shepherd's pie—layers of potatoes, red onions, scallions, green peas, and sautéed turkey, covered with a layer of Jiffy biscuit mix. At most every lunch or dinner Evelyn set out two of Carl's other favorites—corn on the cob and salad.

MEETING THE PRESS

Hundreds of reporters and T.V. crews from dozens of nations searched for him. He agreed to one pre-Games press conference. More than 700 reporters showed up. They fumed and tapped their feet when Carl, always slow in everything except running, came into the hot and crowded room 30 minutes late. He was wearing a red pierced-leather shirt which zipped up both sides. He had decided on a new hairstyle for the Olympics, and for all those television cameras that would send his image to more than 200 countries around the globe. His hair had grown a little longer on top, and was cropped closely along the sides. One reporter, perhaps still seething over that half-hour wait, pronounced that Carl was now a lookalike for singer Grace Jones.

He was still breezily self-confident as he answered questions. A reporter asked if he could have been a success in pro football. He said, with seeming seriousness, that he could have been one of the all-time greatest. That kind of reply prompted one reporter to write that Carl, "like all great athletes, is full of himself." Another wrote: "He is the greatest athlete, and probably the greatest egotist, we have ever seen."

A British reporter asked if he were running in this Olympics for the money he would gain. (His contracts with shoe companies were now reported to be worth at least half a million dollars a year.) Or was he seeking to become a folk hero like Jesse Owens?

ROLE MODEL

"That's a great question," Carl replied with the poise of a diplomat, even though he had been thrown much the same question a hundred times during the past year. "My objective is to be the role model, not the rich man," he said, without adding that he had, in reality, already become both of those things.

Carl refused all requests for one-on-one interviews, including one with a television personality who had been a role model for Carl—ABC's O.J. Simpson. But Carl had special ties to ABC, having worked as a sports interviewer for a Houston ABC affiliate just before the Olympics. In Los Angeles, a few days before the opening ceremonies, Carl had visited the ABC-TV control center for the Olympics. He watched Roone Arledge, the network's sports chieftain, seated in front of a wall of flickering TV sets. From there Arledge would choose the scenes which would go out over the networks on the Evening News. During a pause Arledge turned around in his chair and said to Carl, "Do you want to try it?"

"No, thanks," Carl replied. But he was obviously thinking of a future career as a TV sportscaster when he added, "I don't want to be in the hot-seat yet."

At Olympic Villages, meanwhile, some American track and field athletes grumbled about being penned in while Carl and several other superstars, long-distance runner Mary Decker among them, roamed free outside the Village. Resentment flared into anger when

Carl suggested to a *Sports Illustrated* writer that Edwin Moses, the hurdling champion and sometimes critic of Carl, had not been appreciative of advice Carl had given him. Moses replied that Carl's criticism "doesn't make sense." Then Moses's wife, Myrella, clawed her way into the battle by telling a press conference, "It was Carl who came to us asking how to do things with the public and how to deal with promoters in Europe. And he never said thank you. That's his style, I guess."

ROOTING FOR THE HOME TEAM

The bickering died down as the dramatic opening ceremonies drew attention away from the personalities toward the panorama of the actual competitions. During the first week of the Games, Carl and his fellow track and field athletes—waiting offstage for their time to come—rooted for the American gymnasts and swimmers, who were piling up stacks of gold medals. One night as Carl watched television in the Santa

Monica apartment of Joe Douglas, an unheralded American swimmer, Bruce Hayes, battled to fend off an oncoming West German in the 800-meter freestyle relay. Hayes held on to the lead for another American gold medal.

"I got very excited," Carl told Melissa Ludtke, "probably more excited than I will get for the 100 meters. I was turning somersaults. I was jumping and screaming."

By the end of the first week, their way cleared by the absence of the Soviet and Communist-bloc athletes, Americans had won 30 medals, 23 of them gold. On Friday, August 3rd, the time of waiting had ended for Carl. The time for winning had begun.

GAMES OF THE XXIII OLYMPIAD
Los Angeles, California
July 28–August 12, 1984

Carl flashes across the finish line in the 100-meter race to capture his first gold medal.

The legendary Jesse Owens takes off for gold-medal victory in the 200-meter race during the 1936 Olympics.

Gina Hemphill, granddaughter of Jesse Owens, passes the Olympic torch to 1960 Decathlon winner Rafer Johnson, during the opening ceremonies of the XXIII Olympiad.

Carl holds high an American flag as he runs a victory lap after winning the gold medal in the 100 meters.

Carl sprints to victory in a preliminary heat of the men's 100-meter dash.

Carl approaches the finish line with intense concentration, and wins the first heat of the 200-meter race.

Carl crosses the finish line to win the second heat of the men's 200-meter semifinals.

Carl rounds the turn and heads for home to win the 200-meter event.

Carl readies his landing in qualifying for the long jump finals.

1936 Olympic great Jesse Owens, whose legend Carl has followed, shows his famous form in the long jump, then known as the broad jump.

An Olympic champion in a new role—addressing a crowd during a religious program in Los Angeles. Carl is a member of the Lay Witnesses for Christ.

Carl soars with a leap of 28 feet, ¼ inch to win his second gold medal.

American runners Thomas Jefferson, Carl Lewis, and Kirk Baptiste kneel on the track after sweeping the men's Olympic 200 meters. Lewis won the gold, Baptiste the silver, and Jefferson the bronze.

Flags hoisted in victory, Americans Baptiste, Lewis and Jefferson celebrate on the victory stand.

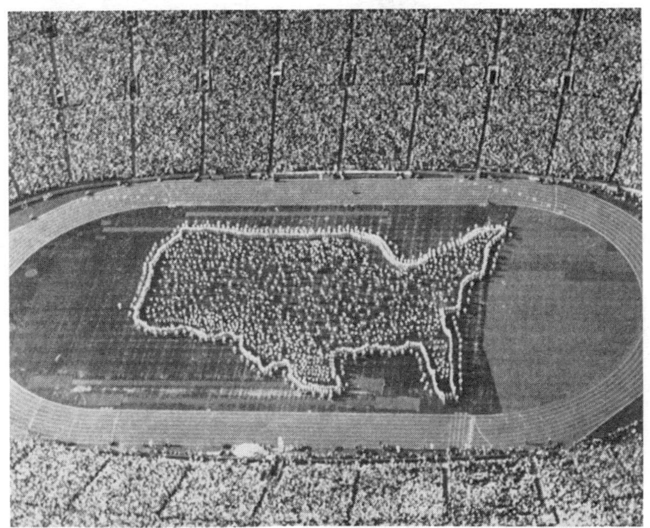

Participants in the colorful opening ceremonies of the 1984 summer games form a shape of the United States.

90,000 spectators filled the Los Angeles Coliseum for the opening ceremonies of the 1984 Olympics.

Calvin Smith provides Carl with a flawless hand-off, enabling Carl to shoot out well ahead on the anchor leg of the 4 × 100-meter relay.

Clutching the baton, Carl dashes across the finish line of the 4 × 100-meter relay and captures his fourth Olympic gold medal.

Carl is hoisted to the shoulders of his 4 × 100-meter relay teammates in celebration of another U.S. victory and Carl's fourth gold.

CHAPTER 9

A TIME FOR WINNING

Clad in red track pants and shirt, Carl walked slowly toward the starting blocks which were set in the white-striped lanes of the track. It was close to 7:00 on a warm, cloudless Saturday evening, August 4th, in Los Angeles. The crowd of nearly 100,000 stared down the track where the eight fastest human beings in the world were lining up to fly 100 meters toward a finish, the possibility of a gold medal, and the unique distinction of being crowned "the world's fastest human."

These eight had survived two heats on Friday and a semifinal just a few hours earlier. The pruning process had sent dozens of national champions—each capable of running a football field in the same time it takes to read ten lines on this page—back to the lockerroom and then to their television sets to watch what might have been. Some of those watching had missed the finals by just a few hundredths of a second, half the blink of an eye.

Of the eight finalists, three were Americans—Carl, winner of both his heats and his semifinal; Sam Graddy of Atlanta; and Ron Brown, soon to become a highly paid pass catcher for the Los Angeles Rams.

Carl took his place in the seventh lane, one lane from the outside of the track. "On your mark!" shouted the starter, gun poised above his head. Eight muscled bodies dipped into the sprinter's starting crouch. "Set!" Up rose the eight on their haunches. In the warm haze the stadium crowd fell silent. The gun cracked, a faraway sound even to those on the track. Moments later the crack was followed by the crowd's rising roar.

Thick legs pistoning, arms swinging, the eight runners charged out of their crouches, at first so smoothly they seemed nonchalant. Then—heads rising to fix on that finish just a straightaway ahead—their charge became one of controlled fury, each stride engulfing one long section of track.

Carl's head came up at 20 meters. He saw that he was no more than an arm's length behind Sam Graddy and Canada's Ben Johnson. At 30 meters the tall figure in red had drawn even with Graddy and Johnson. At 50, he began to pull away from the ragged line which trailed him on the left. Carl shot across the finish line two meters ahead of Graddy and Johnson, winning by one-fifth of a second, tying for the widest margin of victory in 100-meter Olympic history. His time was 9.99, a quarter stride short of Calvin Smith's world record of 9.93 and Jim Hines's Olympic record of 9.95.

VICTORY

Carl ran down the track, arms thrust high, his inner joy reflected—as always when he wins—on his shining face, his stony cheekbones seeming to sparkle.

Carl saw a huge American flag being waved at a trackside box seat. He ran over to the box, where Paul Tucker of New Orleans was swinging the flag. "I thought he was just going to shake somebody's hand," Tucker said later. Instead, Carl grabbed the flag and ran down the track, swinging it in figure 8s as the crowd let out another roar of surprise and delight.

Carl jogged back to Tucker's seat, said "Thanks," and gave him back his flag. Then Carl vanished into a tunnel, where an official asked him if he felt he had made a 25 percent stride toward his goal of four gold medals.

THE SIXTY-PERCENT SOLUTION

"No," Carl said, "as far as I'm concerned, sixty percent of it is over. This is by far the toughest event, because so much can happen in a short race. That's why I get emotional when I win the 100, because it is the most difficult of the four. One bad start, one stumble along the way, and there's no time to get back. You've lost."

On Sunday, August 5th, the third day of Carl's nine-day odyssey, he qualified for the long jump with what was, for a him, a so-so jump of 27 feet, 6 inches. Nevertheless, it was the longest leap by any of the dozen qualifiers.

Monday, August 6th, day number four, would be the most grueling of the nine. It also turned out to be the most tempestuous. In the morning he had to run two 200-meter heats to qualify for Wednesday's semifinals. Carl won both heats, but after the second he felt a tightness in his left leg and he began to worry. Was the hamstring muscle in his leg bunching up?

That evening he peeled off his tight-fitting royal blue warm-up suit for the finals of the long jump. In his mind—and certainly in the mind of Joe Douglas, who had mapped the strategy for making Carl a millionaire superstar—there was the nagging concern that a tightening hamstring could slow down or hobble Carl in the long jump, the 200, and the 400-meter relay. Three potential gold medals could be flying out the window. Carl Lewis would be just another of the literally hundreds of men and women who had won a single gold medal at these Summer Olympics. Carl would be just another pretty face in the crowd. What made Carl unique to advertisers and shoe manufacturers, both men knew, would be those record-tying four golds and the image of "a new Jesse Owens" at worst, "a new Michael Jackson" at best.

There was, of course, Bob Beamon's prodigious record leap of 29 feet, 2½ inches, the distance that a teenage boy had dreamed of soaring. But Carl was no longer a dreaming teenager. Now he was a practical young man confronting the high-pressure world of merchandising. The market price for dreams was next to nothing.

PLAYING IT SAFE

Carl and Douglas decided to play it safe, taking no chance of an injury by going—-unless it had to be done—for Beamon's record and for breaking the 30-foot barrier beyond it. Carl had showed that he accepted this thinking when he said at a press conference earlier in the Games that "...fans like competition. They don't necessarily like records."

Carl and the other long-jump competitors each had six tries. On Carl's first leap he flew 28 feet, ¼ inch, an ordinary jump for him, but the second longest Olympic leap ever, only a little more than 13 inches away from Beamon's best. Carl had hardly warmed up. He still had five more tries in which to make up those 13 inches. Often, in fact, during the past four years he had improved by more than a foot from his first leap to his last.

But on his next jump he fouled. Carl then walked over to the sidelines and pulled on his warm-up suit. He said later that he had felt a twinge in his left leg during the two jumps. Word spread across the Coliseum that Carl would jump no more. Spectators who had paid as much as $100 a seat to watch Carl crack Beamon's record began to mumble.

As Carl watched, other jumpers tried to better his mark of 28 feet, ¼ inch. But no one could come within a foot of that distance. A loud speaker announced that Carl Lewis had won the long jump. The announcement was met by booing from the unhappy ticket-holders. The booing didn't stop even when Carl came out to stand on the victor's platform, the second- and third-place finishers below him. He bowed his head and his second gold medal, dangling from a ribbon, was placed around his neck. The booing continued. Only as the first notes of the "Star-Spangled Banner" rang out across the Coliseum did the booing cease.

Two medals down and two to go, but Carl Lewis didn't win any fans with his performance in the long jump. Nor was his reputation boosted by a statement issued in his name by Olympic officials. The statement said, "If someone had jumped farther, I could not have come back. I was sore after the second jump. That was it."

Most everyone—friends and critics alike—thought that statement curious. Would a soreness in his leg have forced Carl, if someone had gone farther than his mark, to give up a chance for that second of the four gold medals he wanted so badly? Later Carl said that he had been misquoted. He told an interviewer from ABC, "But what I said was that I hoped the jump would hold up, so I wouldn't have to jump again. I would have jumped if a foreigner had passed me."

"BRIEFCASE ATHLETES"

"They're all businessmen in the sport now," veteran high-jumper Dwight Stones, a member of the 1984 team, had said earlier of today's track stars, tagging them "briefcase athletes." Before the Olympics, veteran discus thrower Al Oerter had said, "They're so concerned about what contract they'll get after the Olympics, they're missing out on a wonderful human experience."

Carl had tried to make it clear that he was not one of the briefcase athletes when he said, before the Olympics, "I compete only for myself, my country, and all the glory goes to God." But a *New York Times* reporter claimed that "no athlete has done more preparation and planning to exploit his Olympic fame this year than Lewis." The *Times* writer added, "Lewis is generally believed to have one of the most lucrative shoe-endorsement contracts, but his manager, Joe Douglas, says he is trying to use the Olympics to broaden his celebrity status beyond those who buy shoes."

AN ALTERNATIVE PLAN

Offstage Olympic squabbles seem to set off with the regularity of starter's pistols—and are as quickly forgotten. This one had faded to a blurred and confusing incident just two days later as Carl strode to the starting line on Wednesday evening, August 8th, for the finals of the 200 meters. In the semifinals two hours earlier, Carl said later, his left leg felt stiff. He decided he would bolt out quickly at the start of the 200-meter finals, to take the lead instead of coming up from behind. He hoped that if his leg hurt badly he would, with this tactic, have built a big enough cushion to hold on for victory.

A two-mile-an-hour wind blew into the faces of the eight starters as they crouched in their starting blocks. The gun cracked. Carl swept into the curve and halfway home was clearly ahead of fellow Americans Kirk Baptiste and Thomas Jefferson. He came out of the curve well in front, crossing the finish line a long meter ahead of Baptiste and Jefferson. Carl's time was 19.80—his fastest ever, and an Olympic record—only eight-hundredths of a second off the world record of 19.72.

Most observers thought Carl would have set the 200-meter world record—his first in any outdoor event—if there hadn't been a headwind. Carl himself thought he might have broken the record if he hadn't been thinking about that sore leg. "Because I was thinking about it in the 200 final," he said later, "I went out too hard. I paid the price at the end."

TEAM TIME

Now it was three down, one to go. On Thursday and Friday, Carl joined the other three members of the 400-meter relay team—Sam Graddy, Ron Brown, and Calvin Smith. They won a pair of qualifying heats to become eligible for the semifinals run Saturday morning—day number nine, the last in Carl's crusade.

In his free moments between events, Carl had joined the rest of the Lewis family in cheering on Carol in the long jump. She had qualified easily for the finals, but against the world-champion Rumanians she seemed out of her class. Her best effort, a leap of 21 feet, 1¼ inches, was good for ninth place. The Lewis family story would forever include four Olympic gold medals, but there would not be a fifth.

On Saturday morning Carl and his 400-meter relay teammates won their semifinal to qualify for the final event. That day, August 11th, an unrelenting sun blazed white in a blue sky over Los Angeles, beating hard on spectators and athletes all through the afternoon. At a few minutes before eight in the evening, shadows lengthening in the infield, Carl and his relay teammates jogged onto the track. For Carl this would be his fourteenth competition. But as he talked with the others, teeth flashing white against the wide mahogany face, he looked relaxed and rested. He had the confident look of someone trying to suppress the inner joy of knowing a precious gift is on its way.

Silence fell over the Coliseum as the runners crouched for the first leg, Sam Graddy running number one for the U.S. Starting on the curve, Graddy came into the stretch with a narrow lead for Brown, who in turn handed a slightly larger lead to teammate Calvin Smith. As Smith came out of the curve to give the stick to Carl, a Jamaican and a Canadian pounded at Smith's heels. Breaking from his starting box, Carl leaned back his left arm, curled so that his palm faced upward. Smith placed the stick in Lewis's palm. Carl seemed to blast out as if shot by an invisible gun, a takeoff that propelled him away from his Jamaican and Canadian rivals so quickly that, for a split second, they seemed suspended in a wall of gelatin. He crossed the line some four or five meters ahead of the second-place Jamaican. The team's time, 37.84 seconds, was a world record.

Carl pressed no hands high in triumph. But as he slowed down a few yards past the finish line, he grasped the sides of his head with his hands, as if trying to literally internalize the realization that the journey was at last over, the course run, the precious prize of four gold medals his forever—as they had been forever for Jesse Owens.

SWEET TRIUMPH

The four runners hugged each other. They waved tiny American flags. One larger flag was settled over Carl's wide shoulders. Minutes later the four stood on the victory platform. Carl bowed, ducked his head, and an official placed the ribbon around his neck. From the ribbon dangled gold medal number four. Carl smiled, reached down and gently touched the medal.

The four teammates stood erect as the National Anthem was played, a glowing Carl singing out the words with vigor. Then white-skirted ushers led the winners from the platform toward the track. Moments later, before the crowd could fully sense what had happened, Carl's teammates hoisted him onto their shoulders and he was carried triumphantly from the Coliseum. At least one observer noted that Carl never looked from atop those shoulders to the scenes of the triumph. Indeed, why should he have? Along that Coliseum track he had relished fully the sweetness of being laden with gold. Now he would seek out other triumphs in different places, away from sport. And anyway, he is, at 23, much too young to look back. Not now. But one day, and on many days, he will, of course, and so will we all.

APPENDIX

THE OLYMPIC GAMES

When Jim McKay or one of the other ABC commentators refers to the Los Angeles Olympics as the "Games of the 23rd Olympiad," they are referring to the four-year cycle that marks the celebration of this greatest of all sporting events. The Olympiad is the cycle, not the Games themselves.

In fact, the Los Angeles Games are actually the twenty-first Games, since the scheduled Games of three Olympiads had to be canceled because of world wars. As President Reagan pointed out, commenting on the Soviet boycott of the 1984 Olympics, the ancient Greeks would stop wars for the Games, but in the modern era the opposite has been true.

Three canceled Games subtracted from twenty-three Olympiads should equal just twenty Olympic Games, so why are the Los Angeles competitions the twenty-first? Because special Games were held in Athens, Greece, in 1906 to celebrate the tenth anniversary of the modern Games.

Here is a list of the Games of the Modern Era.

Olympiad	*Year*	*Site*
Ist	1896	Athens
IInd	1900	Paris
IIIrd	1904	St. Louis
	1906	Athens
IVth	1908	London
Vth	1912	Stockholm
VIth	1916	Awarded to Berlin but canceled (World War I)
VIIth	1920	Antwerp
VIIIth	1924	Paris
IXth	1928	Amsterdam
Xth	1932	Los Angeles
XIth	1936	Berlin
XIIth	1940	Awarded first to Tokyo then to Helsinki but cancelled (World War II)
XIIIth	1944	Awarded to London but cancelled (World War II)
XIVth	1948	London
XVth	1952	Helsinki
XVIth	1956	Melbourne
XVIIth	1960	Rome
XVIIIth	1964	Tokyo
XIXth	1968	Mexico City
XXth	1972	Munich
XXIst	1976	Montréal
XXIInd	1980	Moscow (American-led boycott)
XXIIIrd	1984	Los Angeles (Soviet-led boycott)

THE LONG JUMP

The long jump was a part of the ancient Greek Games, at least as early as the seventh century B.C., but in those days the athletes jumped with weights in their hands. No one knows for certain why. Theories about the weights range from a technique of increasing the jumper's forward force at the moment of the jump to an imitation of the conditions soldiers faced in battle.

The long jump has been part of every modern Olympic competition, and, like the sprints, has been very much an American event. In the nineteen Olympic Games in which the United States has competed, Americans have dominated the long jump, winning a total of 36 medals—the gold in all but the 1920 and 1964 Games, when they had to settle for the silver.

Jesse Owens's 1936 Olympic record leap of 26 feet, 5½ inches stood until 1960, when Ralph Boston, also an American, added 2¼ inches to that distance. Boston's record stood until 1968.

In 50 years, the world and Olympic long-jump records had progressed a full two feet. Like most records, the progress had been gradual, at least until Jesse Owens. His standard raised the Olympic record by a foot, but as we've noted, it took another quarter of a century to add just two more inches.

In 1968, at the Mexico City Games, a young man from New York City hit the takeoff board and leapt into history. Bob Beamon jumped 29 feet, 2½ inches in what has been called the greatest athletic achievement ever. He looked at the jump, heard the announcement that he had bettered the world and Olympic records by nearly two feet, and fell to his knees, overcome by emotion. "But it's impossible," he said. "I can't believe it. It's madness, I tell you." Many have confidently predicted that the record will not be broken in the twentieth century. But they don't have Carl Lewis's confidence.

How does anyone—Owens, Beamon, or Lewis—jump so far?

The key is speed. If you can't run fast, you can't jump far. Carl's long-jump run-up covers exactly 57 yards in exactly 23 strides. He reaches a top speed of 25 miles per hour or better. When he reaches the takeoff board, he jumps. Nothing could be simpler, right?

In fact, the long jump is so simple only a physicist can really understand it.

When a high-jumper like Dwight Stones jumps up and over a seven-foot bar, his main task is to fight gravity. He does this by "raising" his own center of gravity as he jumps. In his run-up, he creates a horizontal force which he then transfers into a vertical force as he stops and hurls himself up. Stops? Yes, he stops. He was going forward, now he's going up. Remember Isaac Newton? "For every action, there is an equal and opposite reaction." When a high-jumper runs up and then leaps up, there is a pause in which the forward energy is converted into upward energy. Because he throws up his arms and one leg as he stops, the forward force is redirected upward and joined to the force created by his arms and leg. Then it is as if he were being carried up on a cloud, that cloud being his center of gravity, which has been raised by as much as four feet.

In effect, the long-jumper does much the same thing, except that the speed of his approach to the takeoff is so great that it is impossible to create the same vertical lift. He doesn't want height, anyway; he wants length.

Think of an automobile coasting to a traffic light that is about to turn green. The driver depresses the clutch, drops the car into first gear and hits the accelerator. He continues to coast until the light changes, and then he pops the clutch. In a squeal of tires grabbing the road, he races away. The action of the long-jumper is like this, even though he doesn't ever seem to be in neutral. But, in fact, when his left foot hits the takeoff board and he throws his arms and right leg up, there is actually a moment in which the gears shift and the horizontal velocity of the run-up is modified by the vertical force of the leap.

At the point of takeoff, as the jumper becomes airborne, there is no longer anything he can do to increase the distance of his jump. He's like a speeding bullet—except that, unlike a bullet, he isn't aerodynamically designed to fly. Thus, the jumper uses a "hitch kick" (Owens did one, Carl does two) to control his flight. If he didn't, his body would turn over his center of gravity, which has moved to his waist, and he'd topple head over heels into the sand.

Carl is better than anyone else at extending his legs at landing. Although it looks like he's about to sit down in the sand (if he did it would make for a bad jump, since his seat would be so far behind his feet), his forward momentum throws that center of gravity over his feet as soon as they hit the sand.

Can Carl—or anyone else—jump 30 feet? It is possible, but much beyond the 30-foot barrier may be impossible. There are limits to human performance. Indeed, so much force would be required in a jump that long that in the moment of horizontal to vertical transference, the jumper's leg would probably break.

There are many different styles of long jumping. There's no object such as the javelin or shot to throw—the only thing that must be propelled is the human body, and it's not as easy as it sounds.

An older method is called "the hang." After taking off from the tape, the jumper's arms reach toward the sky, and with an arched back, the jumper points his feet toward the pit. At the point of landing, the jumper's momentum is supposed to drive him forward.

The most commonly used modern method is "the hitch kick." As the jumper leaves the ground, he continues pumping his arms and leaps while positioning his legs.

Other long-jumpers have experimented with rather unique methods in hopes of breaking the laws of gravity. A number of years ago, a New Zealander tried to somersault in mid-air prior to landing. He never approached the competitive 26-foot mark.

One of the first things a jumper must overcome is the natural inclination to worry about breaking his fall. Carl Lewis told *Esquire* magazine about two successful ways to conquer this desire. "One is to throw your arms and legs forward and clutch for the earth like a cat dropped from a high place, always landing on all fours. The other is to sit back and throw your legs out—a kind of feint into a long baseball slide."

In practice Carl rarely goes all out in his jump. Like a thoroughbred race horse, he saves his best efforts for the time an award is on the line. He prefers to isolate the different parts of his long jump—the approach, the flight, and the landing. Carl's coach, Tom Tellez, told *Newsweek*, "Carl uses as much time as possible before each attempt to make a mental movie of the technique he's about to employ."

One advantage Lewis has is the speed he can generate as a world-class sprinter. As Lewis nears the end of the approach, his foot hits the eight-inch takeoff board. He is often traveling at nearly 30 miles per hour.

Lewis uses an approach run of approximately 165 feet, or 22 of his strides. When he was younger, he used a 145-foot approach. As he learned to handle the greater speeds, generated by the additional 20 feet, Lewis began leaping to world-competition lengths. Lewis has the ability to adjust his approach run during a meet. As he told *Esquire*, "Sometimes I'll pick the whole thing up and move it back a bit to avoid fouling at the board, or sometimes I'll move it up if I haven't been jumping well, so that I have to cram the board."

Coach Tellez is a student of physics and kinesiology. According to Tellez, too many jumpers worry about the height of the leap. He says, "The height is dramatic, but you don't go anywhere. You're taking away from the most important thing, which is horizontal velocity."

Tellez has made a study of the body's movements as the jumper is airborne. "When you break contact with the board, your hips, which are your center of mass, form a perfect parabolic curve throughout the jump. We know this; research tells us. You cannot alter that parabolic curve. And I know that they tell me horizontal velocity is a two-to-one ratio, to the vertical velocity, so I'm not interested in getting that much height in a long jump."

So Tellez tries to get Lewis to increase his speed on the approach. He recalled in *Sports Illustrated*, "You have to push the approach while being aware of the coming takeoff. The faster you're moving, the more force you can create in a shorter period of time." According to high-jumper Dwight Stones, "Lewis's speed makes him the class of the event."

As Lewis prepares to approach his leap, he concentrates on the takeoff board and the distant sandpit. With his hands open and loose, Carl begins rocking on the balls of his feet, the left foot in front of the right. When he senses the requisite adrenaline flow, he shifts his weight back, high-steps with his left foot, and begins to run.

As he runs, each stride becomes longer and quicker. Running on the balls of his feet, arms pumping, Lewis approaches the tape of the takeoff board. Like a jet ready to ascend, Lewis looks forward to leaving the ground. "It takes so long to run down the runway. . . ." he says.

Unlike many other long jumpers, Lewis never looks down at the tape as he lands on the takeoff board. With his ability to time his strides, and with his confidence flowing, he almost always hits the eight-inch board perfectly. As his foot lands flatly on the board, he dips his hips, half-steps with his other foot, and up he goes.

Once in the air he does a sort of double kick. Tellez describes it as ". . . a frantic rotation of his arms and legs. This allows him to 'attack' the air and keep from hurtling head-over-heels into the pit."

The double hitch requires the ability to perform intricate arm and leg rotations. "It's a delicate balance to maintain at this speed. If he hesitates at any point, the whole jump will be thrown off," Tellez explains. In *Esquire*, Carl describes his leap as just the second part of his prepared flight. "It's a flow. If I hesitated, number one, I probably wouldn't finish. Number two, my body would tip about two inches forward, and therefore I'd have to fight harder to counteract forward rotation. In order to do that, I'd have to stretch my axes, which are my arms and legs, out more. I'd have to stretch out further than my actual running form, which would cause me to turn sideways just a touch, and I'd land on the side of my body."

Traditionally, Lewis has enough flight time to pump his legs three times. Then with his arms up, he bends to the waist, left leg pointed forward, right leg bent at the knee. After he's approached maximum height, he thrusts his right leg forward. If all goes well, he lands with both heels.

The momentum of Lewis's flight must be broken by bending the knees, causing his body to almost hit the sand. Then, like a gymnast pushing off the vault, Lewis flings both arms to get the forward motion back into the jump. In this way his distance is measured by the point of impact of his feet and not an errant touch of his hands.

All these intricate, carefully calculated flight movements take place in the blink of an eye. "It's so quick," Lewis says, "and I'm so comfortable that sometimes when I get out of the pit I have to ask Coach Tellez if I did it right."

THE SPRINTS

The sprints (in the Olympics, the 100- and 200-meter races and the 4 × 100-meter relay) are probably humankind's most venerable sporting competition. Historians believe that the first Olympic Games in recorded history, held in Greece in the seventh century B.C., had just one event: a sprint of just under 200 meters. The winner of that race was a man called Coroibos of Elis, perhaps the first man to be hailed as the "World's Fastest Human." It is the modern Olympic 100-meter champion who wins that title today.

Since the modern Games began in 1896, Americans have dominated the sprints. In the 100 meters, the U.S. has won the gold in thirteen of the twenty Games in which Americans have competed. Before Carl Lewis's 1984 victory, no American had been the 100-meter Olympic champion since Jim Hines won in 1968. Only twice, in 1928 and in 1976, have Americans been entirely shut out of the 100-meter medals.

Throughout Olympic history, only seven men in addition to Lewis have won the 100-meter/200-meter double. Among them, of course, was the great Jesse Owens, who also won gold medals in the long jump and in the 4×100-meter relay.

Owens's legendary 100-meter victory in 1936, with Adolf Hitler looking on, is one of those Olympic moments that make the Games so exciting and memorable. The winning performance of Great Britain's Harold Abrahams in 1924 was largely forgotten until the Academy Award-winning film *Chariots of Fire* revived the dramatic story of Abrahams and his teammate, the 400-meter champion Eric Liddell. A recent television commercial features the actor Ben Cross, who portrayed Abrahams in the movie, dining with the American runner Jackson Scholz, now 87, whom Abrahams beat for the 100-meter gold, but who won the 200-meter gold. Interestingly, the filmmakers took considerable liberties with the facts. *Chariots of Fire* correctly portrays Liddell's refusal to compete on Sunday, but it suggests that he ran only the 400-meter race, which he won so dramatically. In fact, Liddell also ran in the 200-meter final against Scholz and another American, Charlie Paddock; Liddell finished third.

Going into the 1984 Games, Carl Lewis had a 100-meter best time of 9.97 seconds, just four-hundredths of a second off American Calvin Smith's world record. Carl's time was a "low altitude" world record. But why is altitude a factor in a sprint?

Mexico City—site of the 1968 Games—sits at 7,350 feet above sea level, at which altitude the decreased atmospheric pressure and density offer less resistance to the runner. Some track-

and-field purists believe that world records should not be allowed "at altitude" any more than they are allowed when strong winds behind a runner aid his performance. And it is significant that as of August 1, 1984, the world records in the 100-, 200- and 400-meter races, and in the long jump, were all set at altitude. In fact, each of them was set in Mexico City except for Smith's 100-meter best, which was set in Denver, America's "Mile High City."

If records were allowed only at sea level, who would hold the world records at 100 and 200 and in the long jump? Why, Carl Lewis, of course.

World records are the dream of every track-and-field athlete—although, as Carl Lewis has said, not necessarily in the Olympics, where the first priority is the gold medal.

Jesse Owens did set three world records on his way to winning four gold medals in the 1936 Olympics. He set world records for the 200 meters (20.7 seconds), the long jump (26 feet, 5 1/4 inches), and as the anchor runner on the 4 × 100-meter relay (39.8 seconds). And with his 10.3 seconds time in the 100 meters, he managed to set four Olympic records as well. The 200-meter record stood until 1956, the others until 1960.

But even those Olympic records, set in the midst of Nazi Germany and Hitler's "master race," were not the high moment of Jesse Owens's record-setting career. Earlier, at a Big Ten (then Western) Conference track meet in 1935, Owens set four *world* records in just one day. The meet was held on the campus of the University of

Michigan in Ann Arbor. Jesse, competing for Ohio State, equaled the world record in the 100-yard dash and broke the records for the 220-yard dash, the 220-yard hurdles, and the long jump. In one day.

THE MAKING OF A WORLD-CLASS SPRINTER

What makes an athlete like Carl Lewis a world and Olympic champion sprinter? Obviously, genetics and training are major factors, but in an event like the 100 meters, one that is over in 10 seconds or less, technique is very important as well.

World-class sprinters reach a maximum speed of at least 25 miles per hour. At the start they accelerate, and toward the finish they decelerate. For a sprinter, top speed is like a wall. Long-distance runners, marathoners in particular, "hit the wall"—but they can run through it, because the primary technique of distance running is oxygen conservation. Their events are *aerobic*. But the 100-, 200- and even the 400-meter races are *anaerobic*. Marathoners manage to supply sufficient oxygen to their muscles to keep their legs moving for over two hours, but a sprinter's muscles call for so much oxygen so quickly that it is impossible to keep them supplied beyond a particular point. In terms of actual time, it is about one minute, probably less.

Many factors help to make an athlete fast. Among them is the ability to accelerate, to get quickly to top speed. There is that top speed itself, and, critically, the athlete's ability to maintain it, to minimize deceleration. In a three-man race, for instance, one athlete may accelerate faster than his competitors but because his maximum speed is not as great as theirs, the others will pass him before they reach the finish line. The other two runners may reach the same, greater top speed, but one of them is able to stay at that speed just a fraction of a second longer than the other. He, obviously, is the winner.

Carl Lewis told *Esquire* magazine, "In the 100 meters you can't try to go full speed again after you enter the deceleration period. You can't say, 'Whoops, I'm sorry,' and slow the deceleration pattern down. It's not going to stop. You run to a certain point and then relax. My main objective is to keep smooth and relax. It's amazing how much distance you can make up."

In a 100- or 200-meter sprint (and, increasingly in the 400-meter race), there is no real strategy. The elements of an athlete's speed are simply a flat-out expression of hard work and God's grace.

Genetically, sprinters are gifted with legs that are long in proportion to their torsos and with lots of what are called "fast-twitch" muscle fibers. Not surprisingly, distance runners have more "slow-twitch" fibers. Fast-twitch fibers provide anaerobic ability; slow-twitch fibers provide aerobic ability.

As every coach learns, "You can't put in what God left out." But even the most gifted athlete must also be well trained. The world's best sprinters learn to have great foot speed. It might seem that a long stride is the most important aspect of sprinting technique, but it isn't.

University of Alabama track coach Wayne Williams recently told *Esquire* magazine, "If you watch a film of a sprinter in slow motion and break it down into a frame-by-frame action, you'll see that the sprinter is totally off the track a majority of the time. At one point in each stride, the down leg pushing back and the forward leg coming down, both feet are completely off the ground; the runner has to be erect in order to maintain that kind of motion."

Olympic great Jesse Owens once said, "I let my feet spend as little time on the ground as possible. From the air, fast down, and from the ground, fast up. My foot is only a fraction of the time on the track."

In the movie *Chariots of Fire*, Harold Abrahams's coach teaches him about overstriding. "It's like a slap in the face," he tells Abrahams, and proceeds to slap him. It was true in 1929, and it is just as true in 1984. Too long a stride pushes back the body's center of gravity. Every time the lead foot hits the track a shock is sent back through the body, slowing the runner down.

Furthermore, a long stride takes more time than a shorter stride. A sprinter's power—and his speed—come from the force his legs generate through his feet and into (and off of) the track. It is better to take shorter strides and create that explosive force more frequently. A longer stride covers more ground, of course, but it doesn't get a sprinter to the finish line sooner.

A sprinter's stride mustn't be too short,

either. The best sprinters have just the right stride; it covers the right distance with the most power and the least shock. Great athletes like Jesse Owens and Carl Lewis appear to be almost gliding. Their technique is held together by the most important factor we've yet to mention: relaxation.

Carl Lewis is so thoroughly in control that he can actually "let go" of himself in a sprint. He remains relaxed right through the last 50 meters, when other runners' muscles would probably start to bind. His relaxation while running is so total, he says, that he must make sure he goes to the bathroom before each race.

CARL'S FAITH

When Carl met Jesse Owens in 1971, the former Olympic champion told the ten-year-old boy: "Determination will being its rewards." Carl admits that those words were very important in his life, both on and off the track.

Determination is the result of positive thinking, and Carl fuels his positive attitude by striving for excellence. Determination is the power to do what others say can't be done, including jumping beyond the 30-foot barrier.

"Every day," Carl told Jeanne Anne Dunn of Robert Schuller's *Possibilities* magazine, "I meet people who tell me it can't be done. They're not believing in what I believe I can do. So I have to just do what I feel I'm capable of. I wasn't getting much encouragement before, but now I am. Just because I might not jump 30 feet next week, does not mean I can't do it. A positive attitude is the most important part of athletics. Right now I may not be able to do everything I want to do, but I feel that someday everything I can conjure up, I can do."

Carl became a Christian in 1981—appropriately, at a track meet. For him, being a Christian simply means being the best he can be. Carl is frank about the role the Lord plays in his life: Jesus Christ is everything to him.

Relaxation is critically important for an athlete, and Carl has found it, in part, through his faith and through the ministry of Lay Witnesses for Christ, which he says helped him to realize that his talent is God-given.

Carl's interest in worldly possessions is well known, but as *Newsweek* noted, "Lewis remained true to his Christian roots, even going so far as to occasionally cover his Nike tank top with a Lay Witness for Christ T-shirt prior to a TV interview."

Some athletes have criticized Carl for raising his arms in victory even before he crosses the finish line, but he is only "cherishing the moment with the crowd." Like Eric Liddell, the Scotsman who won the 400-meter gold medal in 1924 and was the hero of *Chariots of Fire*, Carl runs with God. As Liddell would say, "When I run, I feel His pleasure."